# Happy About My Resume

## 50 Tips for Building a Better Document to Secure a Brighter Future

### Barbara Safani

20660 Stevens Creek Blvd., Suite 210
Cupertinom CA 95014

First Printing: October 2008
Paperback ISBN: 1-60005-112-X (978-1-60005-112-8)
Place of Publication: Silicon Valley
Paperback Library of Congress Number: 2008936651

eBook ISBN: 1-60005-113-8 (978-1-60005-113-5)

## Trademarks

All terms mentioned in this book that are known to be trademarks or service marks have been appropriately capitalized. Happy About® cannot attest to the accuracy of this information. Use of a term in this book should not be regarded as affecting the validity of any trademark or service mark.

## Warning and Disclaimer

Every effort has been made to make this book as complete and as accurate as possible, but no warranty of fitness is implied. The information provided is on an "as is" basis. The authors and the publisher shall have neither liability nor responsibility to any person or entity with respect to loss or damages arising from the information contained in this book.

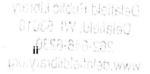

# Endorsements

*"'Happy About My Resume' is an excellent guide to creating the perfect resume. Barbara is considered a top resource for job searchers in NYC and has shared her wealth of knowledge in this book. The resume is an essential part of any job search and Barbara's step-by-step approach helps to build a resume that will attract the attention of recruiters. With easy to follow tips, great samples and clear job search tips - every job seeker should have a copy!"*
**Brian McComak, MSM, PHR, Director, Human Resources, L'Oreal**

*"Happy About My Resume is the book you need by your side as you prepare your own resume. Barbara walks through every aspect of a resume with important issues that come up and masterfully addresses best practices, with real examples. I think these tips and secrets are exactly what professional resume writers don't want you to learn!"*
**Jason Alba, CEO, JibberJobber.com**

*"'Happy About My Resume' is a down-to-earth, practical resource to help you create a resume as compelling as you are. Barbara gives straightforward advice about how to articulate your accomplishments and present them for today's busy hiring manager. Her 50 Tips tell you precisely how to craft your own powerful marketing tool from headline to footer."*
**Liz Sumner, Director, Career Management Alliance**

*"A 'solid read'. 'Happy About My Resume' gives its readers many examples of constructing their resume and backs it up with solid, thorough advice. Those who follow will benefit."*
**Timothy Finney PHR, CSP Regional Manager, Superior Staff Resources, Inc**

*"Barbara has written a career navigational tool that transcends industries and professional levels. She helps the resume writer take a step back, cut to the chase and deliver a real picture of their skills, knowledge and abilities. I am giving this book to clients and students because Barbara's unique, truthful approach and style will aid them in their career journey."*
**Jeanne Stewart, SPHR, President, Human Resources Association of New York, President, HR on the Move, LLC.**

*"Barbara makes a complex topic very clear and concise. Her thorough understanding of the subject matter helps the reader understand what and how they need to go about crafting a strong and salable resume. Her suggestion that the resume is a sales tool is 100% accurate. As a retained executive search consultant, this is the type of book I would recommend that many candidates should read before they commence their job search."*

**Allen A. Geller, Managing Director, Raines International, Inc., http://rainesinternational.com**

*"In a competitive field, Barbara is able to offer exceptional clear, concise and practical job seeking advice. Coming from executive search, I often hear career counselors provide academic recommendations that may work in academia, but do not translate into corporate America and gain the attention of hiring managers. Barbara never misrepresents but finds a way to bring out the best in everyone personally and professionally. Her keen advice can impact all industries and levels. A must-read for any job seeker!"*

**Lorri Zelman, Managing Director, Human Resources Practice, Solomon Page Group**

*"This book is worth the introduction alone. Barbara presents a real-world and step-by-step overhaul on the resume that everyone wrote 20 years ago and has been suffering with ever since. Straightforward and crystal clear, it is a much-needed wake up for any serious job seeker. If a fraction of the resumes that crossed my desk included what is in this book, most of those people would be hired and retained long term."*

**Chason Hecht, President, Retensa Retention Experts, http://retensa.com**

*"I'm not surprised that Barbara Safani has such a fantastic approach to making the resume development process something that a frustrated job seeker can be 'happy about'. As CDI's former Director of Resume Certifications and a multi-resume competition award contributor and judge, Barbara has provided excellent advice in the form of informative and strategic tips for introducing your candidacy, formatting, and creating dynamic experience sections.*

**Laura DeCarlo, President, Career Directors International, http://careerdirectors.com**

## Dedication

This book is dedicated to my daughter, Maia, whose drive and commitment for what she is passionate about continues to inspire me; my son, Darius, who always reminds me that life is like a roller coaster and that is what makes it so much fun; and my husband Al, the squeaky wheel, who kept after me to write a book and didn't let up until it was done.

## Acknowledgments

I'd like to thank Wendy Enelow, Louise Kursmark, and Deb Dib for being pioneers in the careers industry and graciously sharing their knowledge and advice with me throughout my career as a resume writer and career strategist. In addition, I'd like to thank all of the talented resume writers who shared samples of their work for this book. I'd also like to thank Jason Alba for introducing me to the Happy About family.

# A Message from Happy About®

Thank you for your purchase of this Happy About book. It is available online at http://happyabout.info/myresume.php or at other online and physical bookstores.

- Please contact us for quantity discounts at sales@happyabout.info
- If you want to be informed by e-mail of upcoming Happy About® books, please e-mail bookupdate@happyabout.info

Happy About is interested in you if you are an author who would like to submit a non-fiction book proposal or a corporation that would like to have a book written for you. Please contact us by e-mail editorial@happyabout.info or phone (1-408-257-3000).

Other Happy About books available include:

- Internet Your Way to a New Job
  http://happyabout.info/InternetYourWaytoaNewJob.php
- Blitz The Ladder
  http://happyabout.info/blitz.php
- Communicating The American Way
  http://happyabout.info/communicating-american-way.php
- Rule #1: Stop Talking!
  http://happyabout.info/listenerspress/stoptalking.php
- I'm on Facebook--Now What???
  http://happyabout.info/facebook.php
- I'm On LinkedIn--Now What???
  http://happyabout.info/linkedinhelp.php
- Tales From The Networking Community
  http://happyabout.info/networking-community.php
- Happy About Online Networking
  http://happyabout.info/onlinenetworking.php
- Foolosophy
  http://happyabout.info/foolosophy.php
- The Successful Introvert
  http://happyabout.info/thesuccessfulintrovert.php

A Message from Happy About

# Contents

# Preface by Barbara Safani

Over the course of my career, I've reviewed thousands of resumes and less than 1% of them have included content that clearly conveys the job seeker's value proposition or story of success. Most resumes read like job descriptions with responsibilities so mundane and boring I can hardly keep my eyes open. Yet when I speak to people about the work that they do, the majority of them communicate their competencies with passion and pride. Something is clearly lost between what these job seekers know they are capable of and what ends up on the printed page.

Part of my role as a career strategist is to help my clients put that passion about their work on a piece of paper to quickly communicate why they are the right person to be called in for a job interview. Even people who don't embrace every aspect of what they do can articulate what they are proud of and the value their knowledge brings to an organization if they are properly coached.

I wrote this book to teach people how to write better resumes. But beyond that, I wrote this book to coach people on how to get better jobs that meet their professional and personal goals. A strong resume is often the first step towards a more fulfilling career. The content of the resume can directly impact the number of interviews you receive. It can drive the interview, improve the quality of the conversations, and increase the likelihood that you will be considered the best match for the position. A  well-written resume can even help you negotiate a higher compensation package after a job offer is made.

I'm thrilled that you have decided to take charge of your career and that you have selected this book as part of the process. Let's get started!

Barbara Safani,
MA, CERW, NCRW, CPRW, CCM

# Introduction

As a career strategist and resume writer, I have come into contact with thousands of people who perform miracles at work every day. They pour their heart and soul into their work and offer their employers their knowledge and skills to help make those companies a success. But you would never know it if you looked at the resumes most people write for themselves. People can usually articulate what they do, but they generally don't convey why what they do is important or who derives value from their actions. They neglect to tie their job tasks to impact. They fail to create a compelling argument for why a hiring manager should give that candidate a chance. The reasons for this vary across candidates, but some of the common responses I hear include:

1. I just did my job. I didn't do anything out of the ordinary.
2. Writing about what I achieved would be bragging and I don't want people to think I have a swelled head.
3. I was in a support role and didn't have any impact on the bottom line.
4. I'm really not sure what impact I had; I never got to see the sales information.
5. I achieved things as part of a team; I can't take credit for the whole project.
6. I plan to explain the impact of what I did at the interview.
7. I don't want to write too much on my resume about what I did because doing so will make my resume too long.

8. I just graduated from college and I haven't done any meaningful work yet.

9. I know I had an impact but I have no idea how to quantify it.

10. I was not in my last job long enough to show impact *or* the last company I was with failed and there is little opportunity for me to show stories of success.

Let me respond to each of these objections:

1. **I just did my job. I didn't do anything out of the ordinary.** Companies hire people to create positive outcomes for the company. If no positive outcome is achieved, the person will not last long. Think about what makes you good at what you do or what would happen if you didn't do your job properly. What problems would arise and what opportunities would be lost? Think about the value you bring to the position and the qualities you bring to the job that make you good at what you do.

2. **Writing about what I achieved would be bragging and I don't want people to think I have a swelled head.** A resume is not a list of the things you do or the skills you have. It is a marketing tool and the goal is to entice the reader with enough information to peak their curiosity and get them to ask for more. As long as the information you are presenting is truthful, it's not bragging. Hiring managers may be looking at hundreds of resumes for the same position. They may spend only a few seconds looking at your resume. They are not really reading it, but merely scanning it for relevance, fit, and impact. Your resume needs to prove all these things quickly and with very little effort on the hiring manager's part. If two candidates with similar qualifications present their resume to the hiring manager and one resume articulates the candidate's accomplishments and the other one doesn't, which resume do you think will get the hiring manager's attention?

3. **I was in a support role and didn't have any impact on the bottom line.** Think past the tasks associated with your role and reflect on the impact your job had on those around you and the business as a whole. For example, IT professionals build efficiencies within systems to improve the service to the end user. This allows the end user to do their jobs more accurately and faster. Administrative Assistants act as gatekeepers for their bosses and help prioritize their workload so the boss can concentrate on the most mission-critical efforts. The assistant develops systems and processes that help their bosses save time.

4.  **I'm not really sure what impact I had; I never got to see the sales information.** You do not need to have exact figures in order to show impact. It is appropriate to estimate numbers as long as you can back up those approximations with sound reasoning during the interview. For example, if you know that you streamlined a process that in turn allowed you to create an additional sales cycle or introduce a new product, you should be able to estimate what the increase in revenues or volume would be. If you automated a process that previously took at least 2 hours on average to complete and now it is completed with the click of a button, you can certainly show the impact of your actions.

5.  **I achieved things as part of a team. I can't take credit for the whole project.** Agreed. You should never embellish your accomplishments or take full credit where it is not due. However, you can say that as part of a team, as co-producer, co-author, etc. that you accomplished something and write about the overall impact of the project you were part of.

6.  **I plan to explain the impact of what I do at the interview.** Good luck getting to the interview. Without proof of your accomplishments in the resume, it is unlikely that you will get to plead your case at the interview. Use the resume as the teaser for what's to come on the interview. Give them enough information about your actions and results to leave them wanting more. Don't leave them in the dark and assume they will ask for more if they want it because they probably won't.

7.  **I don't want to write too much on my resume about what I did because doing so will make my resume too long.** You can create impact without being verbose. Concentrate on delivering a key metric and a succinct glimpse of the accomplishment and you will be able to keep the document to a reasonable length.

8.  **I just graduated from college and I haven't done any meaningful work yet.** Perhaps you haven't done much paid work yet, but you've certainly done work that will help you prepare for the next steps in your career. Focus on the accomplishments within your coursework, internships, volunteer positions, and leadership roles on campus.

9.  **I know I had an impact but I have no idea how to quantify it.** Take a look at previous years' performance reviews for indicators of your impact or talk to colleagues about projects you worked on. Impact isn't just about the numbers. Perhaps you introduced some "first-ever" initiatives, mentored and trained new employees,

accepted an interim leadership role, or reversed an at-risk relationship with a client. Discuss the successes within these accomplishments and use phrases such as "significantly improved" or "substantially reduced" to prove impact.

10. **I was not in my last job long enough to show impact or the last company I was with failed and there is little opportunity for me to show stories of success.** You may still be able to discuss projected results or impact for a company where your tenure was short. If the company was struggling, write about what you did contribute. Perhaps you set up the company's first infrastructure or you built the sales pipeline from the ground up, or recruited and trained the staff. Separate your successes from the failures of the company and if possible, back those successes up with quotes from a supervisor or vendor.

Regardless of industry, company, position, or level everyone can prove impact. Everyone who is employed is there to do a job that helps the company make money, save money, save time, grow the business, or keep the business. If they are not successful at doing one or more of these things they will be shown the door very quickly.

When you present yourself as a candidate for an employer's open position, you are generally an unknown and there is risk associated with your candidacy. The resume is the first opportunity you have as a job seeker to prove to a hiring manager that there is a strong match between your skills and those required for the open job. Resumes that simply convey job tasks may match some of the job requirements, but they do little to differentiate you from your competition. Many hiring managers believe that past success is a strong indicator of future success. By showcasing stories of success on the resume that prove you have had a positive impact on the company, you bring yourself one step closer to securing a job interview.

The resume is similar to the frame of a house. Almost everything you do as part of your search strategy is related in some way to the resume. The resume is generally the tool hiring managers use to guide them through the interview. If you have not positioned yourself as a candidate with strong achievements you may not be seen as the right candidate for the position. The impact you convey on the resume will also drive your negotiation strategy during the final stages of the interview process. If you successfully communicate your value add through your accomplishment stories, it will be much easier to justify the compensation you desire later on in the interview process.

An excellent strategy for creating stories of success is to craft challenge-action-result (C-A-R) scenarios.

# Challenge

What challenges, problems, or obstacles did you face in each of your positions? What hurdles did you have to overcome? What was the condition of the organization or department when you arrived?

# Action

What did you do to address those challenges? What did you do to improve productivity, turnaround time, or customer service? Did you initiate a process that saved time or money? Did you penetrate a new market, capture market share, introduce a new product, turn around a struggling business, or increase product visibility? Did you create any efficiencies, cut costs, improve any processes, or eliminate any redundancies? What expectations were set for you at work and how did you perform against those expectations? What did you do better than your predecessor or peers? What are you known for?

# Results

What were the results of your actions? Can you quantify your results using dollars, percentages, or hours? Can you show the before and after picture of your actions and use numbers to prove impact? Can you showcase any examples where you completed projects on budget, on time, or under budget and ahead of schedule? Did you meet the expectations for your job? Did you exceed expectations and if so, what benchmark can be used to prove this?

The C-A-R story is the engine that drives the resume strategy. Create as many C-A-R stories as you can and then you can make decisions as to which are the most relevant for your target job. Strive for at least three to five accomplishment stories for your most recent position. As you move further back in your chronology, you may have fewer stories or even just one overarching accomplishment story that gives your reader a flavor for the type of success you achieved at a past position.

The information in this book is divided into different types of resume tips. Chapter 1 deals with tips for displaying your contact information. Chapter 2 discusses resume tips for introducing yourself on paper to the hiring manager in a way that fosters interest and encourages the reader to read on. Chapter 3 details the important points to consider while writing the chronology section of the resume and offers recommendations for strategies to keep the reader engaged and interested in the content. Chapter 4 reviews strategies for including information on hobbies, volunteer work, and professional affiliations in a meaningful way. Chapter 5 shows you how to leverage a recent college degree to garner attention from a hiring manger. Chapter 6 discusses formatting concepts and rules. Chapter 7 offers information on the dos and don'ts of resume writing. Chapter 8 discusses strategies for creating strong cover letters. Appendix B Includes over 40 resume samples and Appendix C includes sample cover letters developed by some of the leading resume writers in the world. These samples were selected because they demonstrate the themes and tips I will be discussing throughout the book. Use them as a guide and as a catalyst for inspiration as you begin to develop your own authentic and unique resume.

Writing a powerful resume requires time, honesty, objectivity, and introspection. We often become attached to everything chronicled on our resume and sometimes it's hard to let go of the past on our way to a new future. I often compare writing a resume to cleaning out a closet. Sure there are a lot of interesting pieces of clothing in the closet and perhaps you've grown attached to many of these items over the years. But sometimes you have to take a step back and recognize that not everything in the closet fits anymore or is currently in style. Sometimes you have to let go of the old in order to make room for the new.

# 1 Tips for Your Contact Information

1. **Include a professional email address.** This subtle detail speaks volumes about how you project yourself to the outside world. If you created your email address during a time when job search and professionalism was not priority number one (i.e., when you were a teenager or a college student, or when you thought the Internet was just a novelty act), take a look at the address you are using and ask yourself if it markets you as a professional and if it is an address that people will take seriously. Every piece of information on your document should reflect your professional identity. Be sure to use an email address that is representative of your identity. Avoid using addresses that use long strings of numbers or letters. Use some combination of your first and last name and try to minimize the amount of numbers that follow your name to decrease the likelihood of mis-keying for someone who is trying to respond to you. Never use a personal email that could call into question your professionalism such as "partygirl7" or "hacker12" and never include the email address you use under a current employer. Doing so allows hiring authorities to question the ethics of your search strategy and leaves them wondering

if you are conducting your search using company resources or on company time. A great strategy for creating an email address that will always be professional and always make it easy for others to find you is to buy your domain name. For example, by purchasing http://barbarasafani.com contacts and hiring authorities will always be able to find you and you will not be at the mercy of your email service provider. Another option is to use your undergraduate or graduate school email address. Most schools now offer a permanent school email address. In addition to offering a stable and professional address, the school address gives you the added benefit of quickly alerting your audience to your alma matter. This can be a great entrée into a networking conversation with others who attended your school.

2.   **Include appropriate contact information.** If you are rarely home and rely on your cell phone for important calls, be sure to list your mobile number on your resume. Never include a work number on a resume unless you currently own your own business. Audit the outgoing message on your voicemail or answering machine. Make sure you are speaking clearly and slowly and be sure to request the caller's full name and phone number and ask that they reference what the call is about. Avoid using slang or music on your outgoing message. If English is not your native language and you are concerned about potential bias on the part of a hiring authority, consider using a prerecorded message or enlist the help of a friend to record the message. Don't turn the responsibility for creating the message over to a minor in the family. Employers don't want to listen to an outgoing message recorded by your 3 year old daughter or teenage son. In addition, if people in your home other than you will be fielding potential calls from recruiters and hiring managers, make sure that anyone involved in the process is given clear instructions on how to answer the calls and take down the important information. As an alternative, ask that the other people in your home let the calls go to voicemail and retrieve the messages later.

3. **Always include an address.** The lack of an address will raise skepticism from hiring authorities. They may question whether you reside in the geography for their open position or if you are trying to hide a certain aspect of your candidacy. If you are concerned about privacy, consider getting a P.O. box to diminish any skepticism on the employer's part. The exception to this rule is online job boards. When posting for jobs online, I recommend following the privacy features offered by many of the sites and removing your address to protect you against phishing and other scams.

# 2 Tips for Introducing Your Candidacy

4. **Create a resume headline.** Headlines sell newspapers. They can also sell job search candidates. Since hiring managers don't really read resumes, but rather scan them to determine the candidate's fit for the job, help make that fit more obvious by creating a resume headline that tells the reader your professional niche. Examples of resume headlines are Award-Winning Television Executive Producer, Entry Level Public Relations Assistant, or Information Technology Product Developer. Include business environments, distinguishing degrees, or special skills that will be of interest to your reader. Resumes that lack a headline are more likely to be misinterpreted or passed over by the hiring manager because the job seeker has not quickly defined the match between their candidacy and the hiring authorities' open position. Headlines can be changed, depending on the opportunity to best fit the job you are applying for.

---

## HUMAN RESOURCES GENERALIST

Financial Services ▪ Retail ▪ Healthcare ▪ Consulting Firms ▪
Government ▪ Not for Profit

*Dual Master of Arts degrees in Social Organizational Psychology
and Counseling Psychology/Consulting Practice*

---

## BILINGUAL FINANCIAL SERVICES MARKETING PROFESSIONAL

*Marketing Campaigns ▪ Product Training ▪ Client Servicing ▪
Sales Support ▪ Series 7 & 63 ▪ Fluent in Spanish*

---

## CHIEF OPERATIONS OFFICER/MANAGING DIRECTOR/DIVISION HEAD

### Wholesale & Retail Fashion Industry

*Global Change Management ▪ Start-Ups ▪ Turnarounds ▪
Multi-Site Operations*

---

## EXECUTIVE FIXED INCOME PROFESSIONAL

*Portfolio Management ▪ Product Development ▪ Senior Investor
Consulting ▪ Quantitative Research ▪ Credit Analysis*

---

5.  **Add a tagline or branding statement.** Communicate what you
    are known for and where you add value underneath your headline.
    Examples of branding statements include:

---

## WEB DEVELOPER AND ON-LINE BRANDING SPECIALIST

*Combining knowledge of online marketing, branding, consumer
search patterns, and leading-edge technology with visual and
artistic sensibility to deliver Web solutions that generate
sales leads, measure and increase key sales metrics,
and deliver sustainable ROI to shareholders.*

---

> ### TECHNOLOGY PRODUCT DEVELOPMENT STRATEGIST
>
> *Combining expertise in technology, business strategy, and operations to help organizations define product feasibility, identify customized solutions, reduce time to market, and increase ROI.*

> ### AWARD-WINNING CREATIVE DIRECTOR
>
> *Crystallizing the organization's vision through brand-on, strategy-on, and cost-conscious compelling creative electronic, interactive media, and print campaigns.*

> ### RECORDING INDUSTRY EXECUTIVE
>
> **SIX-TIME GRAMMY NOMINEE ▪ GRAMMY NOMINATED PRODUCER**
>
> ***Building multimillion-dollar record labels by promoting authentic niche talent and executing strategic crossover marketing campaigns to create breakthrough hits that increase artist recognition and capture new market share.***

6. **Include a quote from the applicant.** Quotes help personalize the document and give the reader a window into the applicant's thought leadership, knowledge, and passion. They help create a connection between the applicant and the decision maker.

> ### CONSTRUCTION PROJECT MANAGER AND GENERAL CONTRACTOR
>
> Multimillion-Dollar Public, Commercial, Residential, Institutional Projects ▪ USGBC LEED Certified
>
> *"Understanding and implementing budget, scheduling, aesthetics, and technical practices: to balance and proactively manage these components is my top skill."*

> **CEO ▪ COO ▪ PRESIDENT**
>
> **New Business Development ▪ Start-Ups ▪ Joint Ventures ▪ Turnarounds ▪ Exit Strategy**
>
> **E-tailing ▪ Broadcast Retailing ▪ Creative Programming ▪ Contextual Merchandising and Planning**
>
> *"I understand how people express themselves through material goods...I can identify trends, but more importantly, I pinpoint what motivates people to take action on their interests. I study what the individual wants and create interactive formats that encourage community and drive revenue."*

7. **Don't use an objective.** Objectives tell the reader what the candidate wants. Hiring authorities are not really interested in what the job seeker wants. They have a position to fill and are interested in how you can leverage your competencies and knowledge to fill that need. Objectives tend to be loaded with fluff ... personal attributes that while important, are not substantiated within the body of the document. Examples of such fluff include phrases like *Dedicated sales professional with excellent interpersonal and communication skills* or *Detail-oriented accountant capable of working in fast-paced environments.* These descriptions are overused, tired, and boring and they do nothing to differentiate candidates since so many people put the same hackneyed phrases on their resumes. In addition, they lack authenticity and rob the reader of the chance to truly understand the value the candidate can bring to the organization. If you are an entry-level job seeker or career changer, consider using a category labeled Career Target or Career Focus instead. This strategy allows you to target a particular job function or industry without using a stale and useless objective.

> **CAREER FOCUS: SUBSTITUTE TEACHER, GRADES 1–6**
>
> Current Childhood Education Master's degree candidate with theoretical and practical experience in elementary education. Proven ability to engage students, keep learners on task, manage diverse learning styles, and present materials in a fun and creative way. Previous experience managing operations for a small business.

| CAREER TARGET |
|---|
| *Entry-level position in U.S. or abroad where I can leverage my skills in written and spoken German and English/German translations.* |

## Job Target ▪ Financial Analyst

### Profile

- Masters Graduate with both practical and theoretical knowledge of business and financial analysis.

- Success as analyst managing bank loans, creating financial and valuation models, and assessing risk.

- Previous experience as staff accountant; advised clients on capital management, interest expense reduction, business setup, and ownership structure.

8. **Create a profile section.** Hiring managers tend to focus on the top third of the first page of the resume. They may only read on if your profile grasps their attention quickly. Communicate your value-add in the profile section. List powerful and consistent examples of how you help the companies you support make money, save money, save time, grow the business, and maintain the business. Showcase big picture examples of how you do things smarter, faster, and more efficiently. Test the quality of your profile by asking yourself if the profile is the only section of the resume the hiring authority reads is it enough to wow your audience and sell your candidacy.

## SENIOR BUSINESS DEVELOPMENT EXECUTIVE

*Insurance ▪ Reinsurance ▪ Alternative Investments ▪ Financial and Insurance Technology Products*

- 15+ year career building business development relationships with C-suite executives at insurance and technology companies, hedge funds, and broker-dealer firms.

- Over a decade of experience underwriting and brokering sophisticated insurance and reinsurance programs and products for nationally recognized, multimillion-dollar accounts.

- Expertise sourcing, pitching, and closing deals that leverage leading-edge technologies to increase revenues for insurance companies by millions of dollars annually.

## RETAIL SENIOR EXECUTIVE

Turnaround Expert ▪ Brand Vision and Transformation ▪ Global Retailers

### EXECUTIVE PROFILE

- General Manager/Division Head with experience managing all facets of the retail and wholesale environment.

- Adept at returning struggling retailers to profitability by streamlining processes, meticulously monitoring customer pulse, and building pay-for-performanc e sales teams.

- Success reinventing product lines, expanding brand reach, and tapping into new lucrative revenue streams.

- Collaborative business partner with track record for fostering relationships with third party retailers, corporations, vendors, and employees to deliver sustainable ROI and gain new market share.

9. **List core competencies.** One of the first things hiring managers will be looking for is a sense if you have the skill set necessary to do the job. Your areas of expertise should be displayed prominently early on in the resume. Try to use the keywords or phrases that are important to your job function and industry. If you are not sure of what the appropriate keywords are, look for consistent wording and phrases on job postings for positions in your field to better align your qualifications with potential job specifications.

## CHIEF OPERATING OFFICER
### Hedge Funds ▪ StartUps ▪ High Growth

- Operations Risk Mitigation
- SEC Registration/Compliance
- Acquisitions Due Diligence
- Vendor Selection and Management
- Technology Upgrades/Integration
- P&L Management
- Forecasting/Budgeting
- Human Resources Administration
- Hedge Fund Product Marketing
- Investor Reporting
- Client Relationship Management
- Office Openings and Closings

## HUMAN RESOURCES GENERALIST
### CORE COMPETENCIES

| | | |
|---|---|---|
| Talent Acquisition | FMLA, HIPPA, ADA Compliance | Benefits Design/Administration |
| College Recruiting/Internships | Payroll Administration | Policy Writing/Implementation |
| Management Development | EEO and I-9 Compliance | Applicant Tracking |
| Employee Handbook Writing | COBRA Administration | Budgeting/Forecasting |
| Competitive Benchmarking | ERISA Administration | Corrective Action Plans |
| New Hire Orientations | Reductions in Force (RIF) | Staff Management |

## SENIOR LEVEL MERCHANDISING EXECUTIVE
### CORE COMPETENCIES

- Apparel Merchandising
- Channel and Brand Management
- Merchandising Strategy
- Production/SKU Planning
- Competitor/Market Analysis
- Cross Functional Team Building
- Product Development/Launch
- International Licensing Relations
- Vendor Sourcing/Supplier Relations
- Product Standardization
- Inventory Management
- Leadership and Mentoring
- Account Relationship Management
- Purchasing Negotiations
- Costing
- Budgeting
- Color and Trend Forecasting
- Staff Development

# 3 Tips for the Professional Experience Category

10. **Include brief descriptions of the companies you have worked for.** For each organization you were part of, include information on the company including the industry the company represents, size, and revenues if publicly-held. The company description is particularly important if you have worked for new, small, or lesser-known firms. Refer to the company's Web site and "about us" page to secure additional data for your description.

---

*Research Vision Ltd, Seattle, WA, 2005–2008*

*London-based affiliate of JRP Securities Corp, (New York based broker/dealer), providing industry analysis to institutional investors via network of independent industry experts and consultants.*

---

BILLINGS CAPITAL, L.L.C., Austin, TX, 2004 to Present

*Private equity firm managing technology, retail, transportation, and real estate companies.*

---

> Jersey City Legal Aid, Inc., Jersey City, NJ, 2006–2008
>
> *30-person non-profit law firm specializing in providing civil legal assistance to low-income clients.*

11. **List operating budgets, account size, and staff size.** Include information on budget and staff size to help your reader gain a better understanding of the scope of your responsibilities.

> *Peak Revenues: $2.5M • Staff: 40 • Facility Size: 13,000 square feet • Operation open 365 days a year*

> Manage 137 accounts; portfolio includes Diageo, Moet & Hennessy, and Kobrand

> *Manage $50M division with 300 + employees in 45 retail locations across the U.S.*

12. **Minimize descriptions of job tasks.** While it's important to convey a brief overview of job tasks, this information does little to differentiate candidates. Many candidates have experience doing similar job tasks. What makes them unique and memorable is the accomplishment within the task. Spend no more than three to six lines discussing the job tasks associated with each position and save space for more valuable accomplishment-focused information. Place the overview of your role directly after your job title and create a concise description in paragraph form to differentiate the job description from the accomplishments to follow.

> *Acted as business liaison and technology specialist to develop leading-edge efficiencies into existing trade support systems. Supported entire team of traders and trade support specialists in a time-sensitive, faced-paced environment.*

> *Co-managed residential mortgage finance unit with whole-loan position of $5.3B and AAA Private Label & Agency ABS positions of $1.8B for this investment and risk management solutions firm. Developed and managed client relationships and communicated business and operational expectations. Researched and analyzed market trends and recommended strategies to minimize risk.*

> *Managed multiple branded dress shirt product lines from market launch through multi-year runs with P&L accountability for design and production costs and gross margin. Orchestrated four-season development phase, sales samples, and bulk production of designer, private label, and basic business lines that grew from $20M to over $140M in sales volume; directly managed $65M in volume.*

> Provide generalist/special project support as member of ten-person HR team. Develop, interpret, and communicate HR policies and procedures and support client group of approximately 900 employees, affiliates, and retirees. Track and report on various HR metrics including affirmative action, turnover, headcount, and department budget.

13. **Maximize use of accomplishments.** Employers are interested in reading about your accomplishments. Past accomplishments are a better predictor of success than a discussion of job tasks. Accomplishment statements are those that clearly indicate how you help the companies you support make money, save money, save time, grow the business, and maintain the business. Discuss the impact of your actions by describing the before and after picture within the organization and showcasing how you improved a process or introduced a new strategy. Have you met or exceeded quotas or department expectations? Have you completed projects on time or ahead of schedule? On budget or under budget? What are you known for and what do you do better or differently than your predecessors or peers? Can you showcase examples of being a strategist, thought leader, or evangelist for a product or service?

Scrutinize every accomplishment statement and recognize that they are the engine driving the resume. Choose each statement carefully and audit its value towards defining your overall brand.

# Examples

*Make Money*

- **Accelerated profit margins by 30%** with projected sales of $400M by launching seven innovative insurance and POS products in just 3 years.

*Save Money*

- **Cut expenses incurred by temporary staffing agencies by $5M;** consolidated vendor list by 60%.

*Save Time*

- **Eliminated over 30 administrative hours weekly** by authoring and designing 50-page Web-application interface that standardized and automated responses to general support desk inquiries regarding the group's flagship product.

*Improve a Process*

- **Streamlined 10,000-user email list** to improve distribution and accuracy of mailings significantly.

*Reverse an Existing Problem*

- **Reduced product imperfections by 500%** by implementing more stringent controls to improve fabric and product quality; achieved ISO 9002 status.

*Be First to Market*

- **Pioneered *CarpetSafe*® exclusive insurance product for ABC Carpets** offering replacement carpet if original is damaged through general wear and tear or staining.

*Build Relationships/Brand Identity*

- **Garnered $13,000 in grant and donation money** and free publicity for *Furnish Coop* by forging partnership with Corcoran Realtors.
- **Successfully launched $50 million bath and beauty market** despite president's skepticism of products' earning potential.

*Grow the Business*

- **Boosted revenues for online watch distributor from underperforming $12M to over $30M,** with average markup of 18% versus previous 3%, well above comparative distributor margins.

*Attract New Business*

- **Grew female customer base from 15% to 60%** by repositioning merchandising strategy and offering high margin apparel, home, health, and beauty products.

*Maintain Existing Business*

- **Reversed strained relationship with $22B supranational client;** renewed 3 year contract despite internal and external expectations that account was unsalvageable and secured an additional $4B in business.

14. **Begin accomplishment statements with powerful action verbs.** Maximize the use of strong verbs to show increases, decreases, and general business improvements. Eliminate weak phrases such as "responsible for" or "duties included". To convey growth, try verbs like propelled, accelerated, rocketed, increased, drove, augmented, added, maximized, and optimized. To prove a positive decrease, include verbs such as reduced, minimized, trimmed, slashed, and cut. Strive for diversity in your word choices to elevate the quality of the document and keep the reader's attention. Following is a list of action verbs to help you create powerful action-oriented statements.

**A**
Abstracted
Accelerated
Accomplished
Achieved
Acquired
Adapted
Addressed
Administered
Advertised
Advised
Advocated
Aided
Allocated
Analyzed
Answered
Applied
Appointed
Appraised
Approved
Arranged
Ascertained
Assembled
Assigned
Assisted
Assumed
Assured
Attained
Audited
Augmented
Authored
Awarded

**B**
Bolstered
Boosted
Bought
Briefed
Broadened
Budgeted
Built

**C**
Calculated
Cared
Caused
Chaired
Changed
Charged
Chartered
Checked
Clarified
Classified
Closed
Coached
Coded
Collaborated
Collected
Combined
Communicated
Compared
Competed
Completed
Conceived
Conciliated
Constructed
Consulted
Continued
Controlled
Converted
Coordinated
Corrected
Counseled
Created
Crystallized
Critiqued
Cut

**D**
Dealt
Decided
Defined
Delegated

Delivered
Demonstrated
Described
Designed
Determined
Developed
Devised
Diagnosed
Directed
Discussed
Distributed
Documented
Doubled
Drafted

**E**
Earned
Edited
Effected
Eliminated
Empathized
Enabled
Endorsed
Enlightened
Enlisted
Ensured
Entered
Established
Estimated
Evaluated
Evangelized
Examined
Exceeded
Excelled
Exhibited
Expanded
Expedited
Experimented
Explained
Explored
Expressed

Extended
Extracted

**F**
Facilitated
Fashioned
Filed
Filled
Financed
Fixed
Focused
Followed
Forecasted
Formulated
Fostered

**G**
Gained
Garnered
Gathered
Gave
Generated
Governed
Graded
Granted
Grew
Guided

**H**
Halved
Handled
Headed
Helped

**I**
Identified
Illustrated
Imagined
Implemented
Improved
Inaugurated

| | | | |
|---|---|---|---|
| Incorporated | Memorized | Procured | Relied |
| Increased | Mentored | Produced | Reorganized |
| Indexed | Met | Programmed | Repaired |
| Influenced | Minimized | Projected | Replaced |
| Initiated | Modified | Promoted | Replied |
| Innovated | Monitored | Propelled | Reported |
| Inspected | Motivated | Proposed | Repositioned |
| Installed | Moved | Protected | Represented |
| Instituted | | Proved | Researched |
| Instructed | **N** | Provided | Resolved |
| Insured | Named | Publicized | Responded |
| | Narrated | Published | Restored |
| **J** | Navigated | Purchased | Retooled |
| Joined | Negotiated | Pursued | Revamped |
| | | | Reviewed |
| **K** | **O** | **Q** | Revised |
| Kept | Observed | Qualified | Revitalized |
| | Obtained | Queried | Rocketed |
| **L** | Opened | Questioned | |
| Launched | Operated | | **S** |
| Lead | Orchestrated | **R** | Saved |
| Learned | Ordered | Raised | Scanned |
| Leased | Organized | Ran | Scheduled |
| Lectured | Originated | Ranked | Screened |
| Led | Overcame | Rated | Selected |
| Licensed | Oversaw | Rationalized | Served |
| Listed | | Read | Serviced |
| Logged | **P** | Realized | Set goals |
| | Paired | Reasoned | Set up |
| **M** | Participated | Recommended | Shaped |
| Made | Perceived | Reconciled | Shared |
| Maintained | Perfected | Recorded | Shaved |
| Managed | Performed | Recruited | Showed |
| Manipulated | Persuaded | Redesigned | Simplified |
| Mapped | Planned | Redirected | Slashed |
| Marketed | Practiced | Reduced | Sold |
| Mastered | Predicted | Reengineered | Solicited |
| Matched | Prepared | Referred | Solved |
| Maximized | Presented | Regulated | Sorted |
| Measured | Prioritized | Rehabilitated | Sought |
| Mediated | Processed | Related | Sparked |

| | | | |
|---|---|---|---|
| Specialized | Supervised | Tracked | Updated |
| Spoke | Supported | Traded | Upgraded |
| Staffed | Surveyed | Trained | Used |
| Standardized | Sustained | Transcribed | Utilized |
| Started | Symbolized | Transferred | |
| Stimulated | Synthesized | Transformed | **V** |
| Strategized | Systematized | Translated | Validated |
| Streamlined | | Transported | Verbalized |
| Strengthened | **T** | Traveled | Verified |
| Stressed | Tabulated | Treated | Vetted |
| Stretched | Tackled | Trimmed | Visited |
| Structured | Talked | Tripled | Visualized |
| Studied | Targeted | Turned | |
| Submitted | Taught | Tutored | **W** |
| Substantiated | Terminated | | Waged |
| Substituted | Tested | **U** | Weighed |
| Succeeded | Theorized | Uncovered | Widened |
| Suggested | Took | Understood | Won |
| Summarized | Toured | Unified | Worked |
| Superceded | Traced | Unraveled | Wrote |

15. **Front-load accomplishments.** Include the most powerful information relevant to your accomplishments at the front of your sentence to elicit the greatest impact. This strategy makes it easy for your reader to spot your key accomplishments and encourages them to read on.

- **Slashed overpayments to third party marketers by 25%** by creating a database to track all activity with these vendors and ensure consistent reconciliation processes and procedures.

- **Shaved $12M off overhead costs and improved profit margins by 15%** by closing unprofitable factories 6 months ahead of schedule.

- **Halved costs associated with stock and cash reconciliation applications** by consolidating applications into single platform, building in-house solutions to replace vendor relationships, and cross-training staff on both cash and position reconciliations to minimize headcount for back office functions.

- **Contributed to 50% increase in Mediamogul stock** by developing and implementing all advertising campaigns, MSO relationships, strategic alliances, revenue sharing, e-commerce and barter relationships with The New York Times, NCAA, and the Library of Congress.

- **Grew site traffic virally in a 3 year period from zero to an average of one million unique visitors per month** by building an engaging online social community, a leading-edge concept at a time when most Web sites still focused on static content.

16. **Quantify accomplishments.** Use dollars, percentages, and numbers to quantify your accomplishments and validate achievements. Consider the information being presented and decide which number is the most powerful one you can convey. For example, if you worked for a not-for-profit and raised $5,000 more in donations from one year to the next, this dollar figure alone might not be very impressive. But if the $5,000 represents a 75% increase over what was raised the previous year, the 75% is a more compelling figure than the $5,000. If you worked for a privately-held firm and it is inappropriate to reveal revenues, prove impact by discussing percent changes.

- Realized $450K in transaction-based revenue fees, 500 potential prospects, and relationships with 15 new trade system customers in only 14 months by acting as catalyst for strategic alliances with two of the nation's largest soft dollar management firms.

- Grew revenues for a technology information systems firm by $2M and increased customer pipeline by 94% by marketing their automated insurance company processes to national insurance companies.

- Trimmed days off production schedules for each textbook chapter by delivering exceptionally clean copy to the copy chief with virtually no changes to content.

- Cut $2.8M off recruiting costs in just 1 year by launching New York City metro area centralized recruiting center tasked with recruiting and training over 3,800; center exceeded 2007 forecast by three quarters of a million dollars.

17. **Group like accomplishments into categories.** After you develop your accomplishment statements, look for trends within your achievements. Do some accomplishments represent increases in sales while others represent decreases in costs or process improvements? Do many of your accomplishments revolve around leadership or project management? Perhaps your claim to fame is your relationship building skills or your knack for sourcing talent. By grouping accomplishments by theme, and creating category headings within the chronology for each position, you can better communicate your personal brand and value add and make it easier for your reader to follow the accomplishments achieved within each key critical competency.

For a PR/Marketing professional…

---

**BRAND MARKETING**

- Expanded record label's footprint by over 90% in key niche markets including African American, Latin, children, gospel, pop, women, teen, and lifestyle markets.

- Improved product visibility and brand recognition while decreasing ad buys by forging inaugural relationships with high profile media partners CBS, VH1, MTV, and Sirius.

- Accelerated brand's reach by researching and managing media buy options in mainstream and niche music publications including Rolling Stone, Vibe, and Essence.

---

For an HR professional…

---

**PRODUCTIVITY GAINS**

- Realized 15% shift in productivity by revamping performance appraisal process and transitioning to a merit-based compensation strategy.

- Restructured workflow allowing agency to service 74 more clients per day by dividing employees into nine teams with a dedicated supervisor.

- Created employee handbook that significantly increased consistency of policy interpretation and decreased HR administrative workload by 20%.

- Implemented HRIS system that reduced time spent on HR administration by 25%.

---

For a not-for-profit professional…

---

**PROGRAMMING INITIATIVES AND FUNDRAISING**

- Raised 100% of funding for hospital's Bi-Annual Fall Carnival and National Cancer Survivor Day by soliciting in-kind donations from hospital employees and surrounding community.

- Garnered $15,000 in public and private donations in just 7 months to support hospital's pediatric programming.

- Spearheaded diabetes and sickle cell monthly support groups for 15 school-age children; incorporated elements of martial arts, meditation, and cooking projects into curriculum.

- Contributed to improved hospital image by project-managing pediatric emergency room renovation; sourced artist to paint mural, selected furniture, and negotiated fees.

- Upgraded unit's patient services to include free television, video game, and computer access for all patients by securing two grants with total value of $15,000.

---

For a television producer…

---

**PRODUCTION IMPROVEMENTS**

- Pioneered leading-edge show format and transitioned from simple studio show to three-segment show that included field pieces, live remotes, video, and guest panels.

- Slashed camera crew costs by $150,000 + annually by recommending automated cameras.

- Cut post-production expenses more than half a million dollars annually by suggesting use of more adaptable digital beta camera.

- Trimmed studio expenses significantly by negotiating alternative shooting schedules and sharing studio space whenever possible.

---

18. **Create big picture statements of success supported by achievement statements.** If you worked on a large-scale project with multiple milestones, consider communicating the full impact of the project in a themed accomplishment statement and then supply several "mini" accomplishments to show your reader the steps you took to achieve the overall objective of the project.

> Reengineered flawed $225M core systems replacement program and corresponding deliverables for leading financial services company to ensure audit compliance and timely completion of project.

- Assembled team to help CIO and management team develop an expeditious turn-around plan to stabilize the program and reset expectations regarding delivery schedule and cost.

- Developed sequential deployment plan that minimized risk and satisfied auditors by reviewing program portfolio and categorizing projects based on execution health and business criticality.

- Spearheaded creation of a program management office to successfully manage the systems integration moving forward.

> Led multimillion-dollar Sarbanes Oxley application keeping all phases of project on time and under budget.

- Trimmed $220K off phase one alone by effectively managing resources and eliminating need for additional consultants.

- Spearheaded due diligence process; audited ten different applications and developed prototype before launching project.

- Oversaw 25-person senior task force comprised of 10 corporate divisions to define requirements and develop proposal.

- Mitigated risk and corporate liability by developing robust security documentation process in compliance with SOX.

- Act as "go to person" and sounding board for Information Security Senior Manager regarding all SOX issues.

19. **Report employment history by years.** Hiring managers generally expect to see the years you were employed by a company, not

the months and years. Exceptions to this include candidates who have less than 1 year of tenure in a position or students reporting on summer employment or internships.

20. **Do not omit employment dates.** All resumes should include employment dates. Neglecting to do so will raise a red flag with hiring authorities and jeopardize your candidacy. If there are gaps in your employment, a better strategy is to explain any gaps in the cover letter or minimize the emphasis on chronology while maximizing the emphasis on competencies and accomplishments. Prepare an up-front abbreviated chronology that simply lists company name, job title, employment dates, and a brief description of your responsibilities. Follow this section with themed competency sections that convey your achievements across various positions and reference the company where each accomplishment was achieved. (see chapter 6, tip #33)

21. **Focus on past 10–15 years of employment.** Generally, hiring authorities are more interested in recent accomplishments than those achieved over a decade ago. Weight information on your documents towards the past 10–15 years and minimize the amount of space dedicated to earlier work experience. The exception to this suggestion is when your most recent accomplishments are not your most impressive ones or where your goal is to focus on accomplishments achieved earlier in your career. In this case, stick with the abbreviated chronology and demonstrate your value add by presenting competency categories in the order that is most relevant to your career target.

22. **Include testimonials.** A testimonial about your work from satisfied supervisors or clients can add enormous credibility to a job seeker's candidacy. Testimonials showcase the candidate's strengths from the perspective of another person and help validate the candidate's core competencies and accomplishments. They personalize the relationship that the candidate is trying to build with the hiring manager and offer a more intimate look at the value the candidate can bring to an employer.

> *"Victoria proactively takes on her responsibilities and she looks ahead to work on upcoming requirements and tasks. She is able to develop and manage a working schedule that delivers tasks and products on time and to quality expectations."* Supervisor

"Mike stepped in to take over responsibility for an initiative that had been a year in the making and was critical to the continuation of our present and future business. His knowledge of the business and passion for his work were apparent within the first week as he managed to get the business and development teams organized and focused on specific tasks and deliverables." *Kevin Sales, VP, FGS Publishing*

"*You are definitely the 'best of the best', and your efforts continue to amaze me!*" *Supervisor*

# 4 Tips for Additional Value-Add Sections

23. **List appropriate hobbies.** Only include hobbies when they are relevant to your job search or in synch with you target audience. For example, an IT technician might mention his knack for fixing up old cars and an event planner might mention her involvement in community theater. Hobbies can also be used effectively to counter potential age bias. For example, the over 50 candidate might mention that she is a marathon runner or an avid equestrian to imply overall stamina, health, and fitness to dissuade any bias that as an older worker the candidate lacks the necessary energy to do the job.

24. **Include appropriate volunteer experience.** Again, include what is relevant and discuss the competencies gained from the volunteer experience that elevate your candidacy. For example, a career changer seeking an entrée into the healthcare field might mention volunteer work done in a hospital or a technology professional might mention volunteer work he does teaching computer skills to disadvantaged youths.

25. **List relevant professional affiliations.** Include relevant and recent professional affiliations and make special mention of any leadership roles held within these organizations. Showcase examples of how you moved these organizations forward to help promote membership, resources, and the profession overall.

# 5 Tips for Education Section

**26. Include graduation dates.** Sometimes job seekers omit their graduation date on their resume to mitigate the potential of someone discovering their age and possibly using this information to bias their candidacy. But by omitting the date, you may actually be calling more attention to the very issue you are trying to hide because employers may question why you chose to omit the graduation date. They may even assume that you are older than you actually are. Transparency is important in a resume. Smoke and mirrors and omissions can damage the relationship you are trying to build with the hiring authority. Keep it real by including dates.

**27. Don't include GPA if you graduated over 5 years ago.** The further away you get from your education, the less relevance it has for hiring authorities. As you move through your career, hiring managers will use your past accomplishments as the measure of your success, rather than school performance. If you have returned to school to gain the competencies to transition to a new career, then the educational experience has immediate relevance to your target market and should be displayed prominently on your resume.

**28. Include GPA if above 3.5.** If you are a recent college graduate, an impressive GPA can help differentiate you from your competitors. For some employers, success in school is a good indicator of success in their organizations. If your overall GPA is not high, but your GPA within your major field of study is high, consider listing that number instead. For students graduating with a Bachelor of Science degree, include your GPA if it is 3.2 or higher. If you graduated with a Bachelor of Arts degree, include a GPA of 3.5 or higher. List honors, deans list recognition, scholarships awarded, and/or information regarding the school's ranking within a particular academic discipline.

**29. Create a separate category for transferable coursework.** Add a section to your resume listing coursework that is related to your target market. For example, a candidate interested in a position as a journalist might list core classes from their college curriculum including "Reporting Methods" or "Women in Media."

---

**CORE COURSEWORK AND RELATED PROJECTS**

| | |
|---|---|
| ▫ Constructing a Record Company | ▫ Artist Development |
| ▫ Media in America | ▫ Television & Information Explosion |
| ▫ Entertainment Law | ▫ Media Criticism |
| ▫ Public Relations | ▫ Newspaper Journalism |

---

*Relevant Journalism Coursework*

News Writing ▪ Reporting Methods ▪ Women in Media ▪ New Media
Ethics Political/Economic Communications

*Relevant Business Coursework*

Marketing ▪ Management ▪ Accounting ▪ Business Law

---

**30. Discuss school accomplishments that are transferable to a work environment.** As a recent college graduate, many of your key accomplishments were achieved within an academic environment.

Discuss successes within the context of class or group projects, term papers or a thesis, or class ranking. Reference examples of projects that simulate real-life work experiences to prove that you could recreate a successful classroom experience in a corporate environment.

---

**Artist Development** – created a marketing plan for hip-hop artist Jo Jo that was presented to the artist and assimilated into his marketing and public relations campaign.

✓ Recommended first single release that was #1 on college radio for several months.

✓ Pitched re-branding strategy to reintroduce artist to the public with a new image.

✓ Authored marketing collateral including bio and press kit; planned appearances/interviews.

✓ Created artist merchandising strategies and developed logos and samples.

✓ Introduced video concept and picked release date for first three singles.

✓ Advised artist to collaborate with fellow hip-hop artist Missy D.

✓ Suggested alliances with local advocacy groups to promote visibility and goodwill.

---

**Public Relations** – developed a comprehensive mock PR campaign for recording artist Slim Boy.

✓ Launched PR campaign with coverage on MTV, BET, and local hip-hop radio stations.

✓ Created themed New Year's Eve event in New York's Bryant Park with an all-night party following record release.

✓ Wrote articles and headlines to promote event and market artist to radio stations.

*Class Project Highlights*

**Construction Edge** Part of a team that developed and pitched a software product that leveraged cell phone technology to streamline building process and minimize downtime between contractor projects. Recognized as only project in class that was selected for actual implementation by investors.

**Pink Network** (women's' television network in Canada) Co-created Web site re-branding campaign projected to shift viewership to younger demographic.

**MASA Magazine** (art and social commentary magazine) – Created detailed business proposal for non-profit magazine that analyzed online marketing strategy and Web analytics and recommended traffic growth plan for site.

31. **Include internships.** Paid and unpaid internships offer students the opportunity to gain valuable experience that is easily transferable into an entry level position. As always, be sure to focus on achievements over job tasks.

*Intern, Liberty Science Center, Jersey City, NJ, Summer, 2007*

- Contributed to 25% jump in membership over a 9 month period by redesigning and direct-mail marketing new membership brochure.

- Designed from original concept development to execution, in-house graphic design department's first-ever corporate identity campaign and associated collaterals.

- With virtually no budget or resources, designed inaugural quarterly calendar that was recognized by senior management as aesthetically pleasing, functional, and on-brand.

- Successfully implemented exhibition graphics for special installments and designed templates for special exhibition brochures despite strict budgetary constraints.

*Fashion Design Intern, Lily Fashions, New York, NY, Summer, 2007*

- Photographed 75 ensembles for design house in conjunction with New York Fashion Week.

- Organized and purchased fabric and trim for model boards.

- Dressed 15 models for fashion show and worked behind the scenes to support modeling/design staff.

- Monitored, tracked, and packaged celebrity loan outfits.

# 6 Tips for Formatting

**32. Use traditional fonts.** Use traditional fonts that are likely to be part of most people's software programs so the document formatting remains consistent when sent to someone else for review. Times New Roman, Helvetica, Arial, Arial Narrow, and Tahoma work well on resumes. Avoid overly ornate or script fonts.

**33. Choose the appropriate resume style for your situation.** Whenever possible, I recommend using a reverse chronological format for your resume. This format is characterized by a historical timeline that begins with the most recent experience and works backwards. This is generally the preferred style of recruiters and hiring managers. For career changers, job seekers with employment gaps, people trying to refocus on skills used earlier in their career, and job seekers returning to work after time off, the chronological format may not be the best option. In this case, use a chrono-functional hybrid style which includes an abbreviated chronology and instead focuses on themed categories of transferable competencies.

# Career Highlights

## Online Gaming

- Successfully pitched concept of offering online gaming servers in Los Angeles market to senior executive at XYZ Cable to help extend product's reach and build list of new subscribers.

- Garnered hundreds of thousands of dollars in revenues and captured new market share for XYZ Cable by spearheading and managing company's first online gaming servers in Los Angeles market.

- Created XYZ Cable's online gaming administrative infrastructure including server setups, game downloads, Web content, layout, and administrative checks and balances. Recruited online gaming experts to manage site moving forward.

- Exceptional user knowledge of *Everquest* and *World of Warcraft (WOW)*; strong personal ties to the online gaming community.

## Record Producer

- Produced hundreds of record remixes for dozens of international, multiplatinum dance, urban, and underground recording artists.

- Launched a private label recording company specializing in underground dance music. Tracks were included in various compilation albums including Boy to Boy's *Essential Gold*.

- Accelerated record distributions and sales tenfold in just 1 year and quickly expanded to international markets that included Japan, Brazil, Australia, and Greece.

## Live Disc Jockey

- DJ'd at world renowned venues including Copacabana, Avalon, and Roxy.

- Well-known DJ in the Boston club scene in early to mid-1990s with regular gigs at Venus de Milo, Axis, Paradise, M80, and Joy.

| | |
|---|---|
| **ONLINE GAMING CONSULTANT,** XYZ Cable, Los Angeles, LA | 1999–2003 |
| **CLUB DISC JOCKEY,** multiple international locations | 1992–2003 |
| **OWNER AND RECORDING ARTIST,** Flow Jam Records, various locations | 1994–2001 |
| **PRODUCER,** X-ing Productions, Boston, MA | 1993–1998 |
| **CLUB PROMOTER,** PaulCo. Productions, Boston, MA | 1992–1996 |
| **RADIO DJ,** KISS 108, (WXKS) Boston, MA KIX106; (WWKX), Providence, RI | 1992–1996 |
| **DISC JOCKEY,** multiple east coast venues | 1992–1996 |

34. **Use appropriate font size.** Use a font size of ten to twelve points in order to make the document easy to read.

35. **Keep your margins between .6 and 1.0.** If you use smaller margins, you run the risk of having part of your document cut off if a hiring manager makes photocopies. In addition, if you reduce your margins to less than .6, the format may not be preserved on the receiver's end.

36. **Use white space effectively.** While compelling text is a critical component of a successful resume, many search candidates make the mistake of cramming too much text into the document. A long list of bullets with no space in between looks like one big paragraph and nothing will stand out. Avoid this mistake by creating white space in between category headings, employment descriptions, and lists of accomplishment statements. A .6 space in between bullets will do the trick.

37. **Include contact information on page two.** If your document is more than one page, make sure your name is on all subsequent pages in case the pages become separated. Consider writing "continued" at the bottom of page one to alert your reader that there is another page to follow and repeat your phone and email address on page two.

38. **Use bolding to grab the reader's attention.** Bolding can help accentuate key facts, numbers, company names or notable competencies. Always use bolding sparingly, so it does not overwhelm the reader or lessen the desired impact.

**39. Don't bullet more than five items in a row.** Too many bullets in a row look like one large paragraph and defeats the purpose of the bullet which is to make something stand out. Hiring authorities, who are more likely to scan your document than read it, are more likely to pay attention to your resume if the information is presented to them in digestible sound bites rather than big blocky paragraphs.

For a telecommunications professional...

---

*Cost Savings*

- **Completed 10 optical service launches on time and saved previous overrun costs of $50M** by improving project documentation and diversifying team resources.

- **Eliminated close to $750K in service order rework and contract penalties** by implementing pre-launch performance and equipment testing initiative.

- **Slashed service overview training expenses by $250K** by utilizing existing in-house training products and hosting virtual technology seminar for 30 team members.

*Business Process Improvement*

- **Identified and resolved close to 200 servicing issues annually** by creating action plan register and holding team members accountable for resolution.

- **Improved functional launch team's credibility and efficiency exponentially** by expanding team size from 8 to 25, tracking action items and critical issues more judiciously, and assigning subject matter experts to specific projects to enhance product delivery.

- **Decreased post-launch support needs by 25%** by creating reporting tool for senior management that communicated deployment issues, improved quality, and kept team on track for on-time delivery.

*Leadership Initiatives*

- **Significantly reduced team conflict and broke down departmental silos** by restructuring meeting formats, increasing communication vehicles, documenting service gaps and mediating disagreements.

- **Nominated for V-tech Excellence Award and rated in top 10%** among peer group as an emerging talent in the organization.

- **Certified IT Project Management Adjunct Professor,** New York University.

---

For a Retail Bank Branch Manager...

### Business Development

- Top producer in region for referrals with twice as many referrals as branch in #2 spot.
- Ranked #1 in investment and multiple service household growth out of 25 branches.
- One of top three producers for check card usage with increase from 59% to 67% in 2007.
- Accelerated consumer lending volume 400% during tenure.
- Bolstered online banking usage from 37% to 48% in 15 months.
- Grew non-interest income categories by 31.5% over 2 years.

### Process Improvement

- Designed and launched company's first automated branch sales tracking system that was implemented nationally in 330 branches. Standardized methods for tracking sales, referrals, and account activity, rewarded successful sales, and identified growth opportunities.
- Spearheaded and facilitated 30hour consumer loan program training for branch that was expanded to 25 locations.

### Relationship Management

- Boosted customer service scores by 15 points and maintained service ratings of 95% or higher over six quarters.
- Received consistent 100% client servicing scores in 2005.

### Staff Development

- Mentored new assistant manager, now a top producer.
- Recruited and trained five tellers and customer service representatives with virtually no turnover.
- Created and led weekly customer service role plays for staff focusing on specific area of relationship management.
- Organized morning and afternoon "huddles" to discuss daily focus and accomplishments.

### Company Awards

- Recognized with *Share of Wallet Award* for referrals to various business lines.
- Received first place award for multiple service household growth and service excellence.
- Presented with *Community Service Award* for various community activities including teaching economics-based curriculum to K-7 graders in conjunction with Junior Achievement.

**40. Use color appropriately.** Depending on your profession, adding color to your document text can add polish to your overall presentation. Color, when done tastefully, can work well for candidates in a variety of fields including fashion, marketing, sales, education, and the arts. For resumes in more traditional fields, such as finance, operations, or government, black and grey are more appropriate color choices.

# Rebecca Small

65-35 JUNO STREET ▪ FOREST HILLS, NY ▪ C: 917-339-4548 ▪ *REBECCA@SMALL.NET*

## AWARD-WINNING CREATIVE DIRECTOR

*Crystallizing the organization's vision through brand-on, strategy-on, and cost-conscious compelling creative electronic, interactive media, and print campaigns.*

- Twelve years' experience managing creative teams to deliver Web/print material that re-brand organizations, elevate public awareness of products and services, and recruit top talent for the organization.

- Proven success building value-added support service models from scratch that are client-centric, reliable, cost efficient, and revenue driven.

- Expertise translating client vision into marketing collateral that are content rich, visually appealing, functional, and easy to navigate.

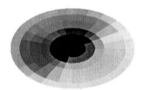

*"Color is about a feeling. It is an extension of one's personality and identity. It can change a person's outlook on life and help them express their hopes and dreams. Color is an integral part of life."*

# LISA M. CHRISTIE

*52-41 37th Street ▪ Astoria, NY 11102*
*lisachristie@yahoo.com ▪ Cell: (347) 866-1212*

## PROFILE

Award-winning, nationally recognized Color Expert with extensive experience in exterior and interior color design for commercial, institutional, and residential properties and strong knowledge of color trend strategies for fashion and design. Knack for introducing color palettes that create functionally appropriate and aesthetically pleasing color schemes for fashion and work/living spaces. Ability to recommend color choices for building materials, paint, wall coverings, floors, tiles, furniture, and window treatments that accentuate strengths while minimizing shortcomings. Strong background in operations, sales, marketing, and management.

**41. Use images or graphs to create a compelling value proposition.** If you plan to bring a portfolio of your work to interviews, consider spicing up your resume with some images of the type of work that you do. Even if you aren't in an artistic field, images can often be used to effectively get your point across. Or use charts, graphs, or diagrams to create a visual representation of the impact you have achieved.

## MARKETING COMMUNICATIONS DIRECTOR

*Creating the connection between a brand's value proposition and the print, online, and experience media campaigns that strengthen global brand equity and drive customer loyalty.*

### Four-Year Business Growth 2004–2007

| NY Branch | 2004 | 2005 | 2006 | 2007 |
|---|---|---|---|---|
| Revenue | $15M | $20M | $27M | $30M |
| Market Share | 15% | 22% | 35% | 46% |
| Client Retention | 82% | 89% | 93% | 97% |
| Referral Business | 10% | 21% | 45% | 72% |

# ALISA V. SIXSMITH

159 Amsterdam Avenue ■ New York, NY 10023 ■ 212-822-5151 ■ six@gmail.com

"A teacher affects eternity; he can never tell where his influence stops."
Henry Brooks Adams

**CAREER TARGET: HUMANITARIAN ASSISTANCE:
GRANT WRITING AND FUNDRAISING**

42. **Proofread for typos and grammar.** Nothing will kill a candidate's chances for an interview faster than a typo or blatant grammatical error. Consider purchasing *The Gregg Reference Manual* to confirm that your document follows the general rules of grammar. For spelling, always use the spell check feature, but don't rely on it solely. Additional ways to catch spelling errors include putting your document down and returning to it several times with a fresh pair of eyes, asking someone else to proofread the document, or reading the document backwards, which forces you to slow down and makes it less likely for you to miss errors.

# 7 Tips for Resume Etiquette

**43. Omit "references available upon request."**
It is understood that candidates will provide references when asked. In today's world, search engines make references available whether the employer requests them or not, and more and more employers are leveraging search engines, social and business networking, and identity management tools to source the good, the bad, and the ugly on candidates. Take control of your online presence by auditing your online professional identity and save the space on your resume for more compelling, accomplishment-driven information.

**44. Use regional spelling if applying for positions in another country.** If you are applying for a position in another English speaking country such as England, Canada, or Australia, you need to be cognizant of the fact that certain words are spelled differently in these countries.

**45. Keep technical jargon to a minimum.** While it is important to include industry specific keywords on your resume, be careful not to include excessive jargon in the document. Jargon can alienate your audience and make it difficult for your reader to understand the context of the jargon or its value to the organization.

46. **Don't include a picture and don't include personal information.** Introducing a visual component to your candidacy is not generally welcomed in the U.S. market. Adding a picture to your resume introduces potential bias and hiring managers are wary of resumes that contain pictures. In the U.S. market, it is illegal to use information regarding age, birth country, ethnicity, religion, or marital status to make a hiring decision. To be considered a savvy candidate in the U.S. market, it is recommended that this information be removed from the document.

47. **Use a high quality resume paper and print your resume on the correct side of the resume paper. Don't staple resume pages.** To ensure a professional look and feel for your document, be sure to use a good quality resume paper. It is generally recommended that job seekers choose muted paper colors such as white, off white, beige, or grey. Quality resume paper contains a watermark that can be seen when held up to the light. Be sure that the watermark is positioned face up and right-side up on the document. It is not uncommon for hiring authorities to make copies of your document to present to potential decision makers. If sending a hard copy, be cognizant of their needs and use a paper clip rather than staples to secure the pages of your document.

48. **Don't fold your resume and use an envelope that matches your resume paper.** If you are sending your document by mail, send it in an 8 1/2 X 11 envelope. The large envelope serves many purposes. It creates a more professional look, improves the likelihood that the document will be scanned correctly, and makes the document easier to find in a pile of letters in standard mailing envelopes.

49. **Save your resume under an easy to locate file name.** Hiring authorities receive hundreds of resumes and many of them are simply called "resume.doc." This forces the hiring manager to spend time saving the files with a more distinguishable title. Choose a file name that includes your last name, first name, and the word resume. This will save the hiring manager valuable time and frustration.

50. **Create a text only version of your resume.** Word documents are not transferable to the text boxes used in many online posting sites. If you attempt to copy and paste a Word document into a text box or the body of the email, the document's formatting is severely compromised. Another advantage of the text version is that you can quickly add it to the body of your email to a hiring manager in addition to attaching your Word version. Having your information in the body of the email can increase the likelihood that the hiring

manager will review your document first because they are not required to take the time to open up your Word document and there is no risk of catching a virus from the text-only version. Here's how to create a text-only version of your resume.

- Save the document in .txt format

- Save document as text with line breaks

- Remove tabs, columns, and bullets and save document with line page breaks

- Set document page at 60 characters per line

- Omit bolding, italics, and underlining

- Check for any symbols that were inadvertently changed during the conversion process (e.g., apostrophes may have converted to question marks)

- Change double quotes to single quotes

- Use spaces to line up text instead of tabs in document

- Add white space or use the ——key to better distinguish text

```
MICHAEL FICKENWIRTH
1321 York Avenue
New York, NY 10021
212-588-1336
917-688-3489


ASSOCIATE TRADER

Emerging Market Bonds, Equities, Futures
* Ten years' experience troubleshooting and recon-
  ciling trade, settlement, and pricing issues.
* Proficiency tracking trades and importing into
  Bloomberg and Microsoft Excel.
* Success managing multiple daily deadlines in
  time-critical, volatile, high-volume environments.
* Series 7 license.
```

# 8 Tips for Creating Value-Add Cover Letters

1. **Use a compelling subject line.** When emailing a resume, you are more likely to grab the hiring authority's attention and elicit a call to action if the subject line of your email includes a memorable subject line such as *Fortune 500 CFO, Five-Time Webby Winner Design Strategist*, or *Six Sigma Project Manager*.

2. **Begin your cover letter with a compelling statement.** Rather than starting your cover letter with a reference to the position you are applying for, write a statement that aligns you with the organization, industry, or job function you are targeting. Discuss an industry problem or need and prove that you are part of the solution.

Dear Mr. Arnold:

A survey by *TopCap Investors* of 200 plan sponsors identified the top factors for choosing a transition manager. Trading capacity and the manager's ability to find liquidity from many large and diverse sources was number one, followed by cost containment, stellar project management skills, a keen ability to identify and deter portfolio, operational, and business risk, analysis and reporting capabilities, and unwavering integrity.

With 4 years' experience providing market structure expertise in institutional sales environments including The Blythe Fund, GMG and Letrue Limited, and a 15-year track record of building and leading sales trading desks for such reputable firms as HSBC, Morgan Stanley, and Marthe Securities, I have built a knowledge base that supports the key competencies of a successful Transition Manager and makes me a valuable asset to a firm seeking someone to fill this critical role.

---

Dear Mr. Daley:

The Internet has brought people together in an effort to connect, exchange ideas, and offer products and services. With the advent of the technology, everyone is using Web marketing. With so much noise in cyberspace, it is a challenge to position a product or service so the prospective buyer can be receptive to your marketing message.

---

Dear Mr. Peters:

The most successful sales representatives are the ones that build relationships, establish trust, and convey authenticity in themselves and the products they represent. As a former social work professional, I needed to meet similar criteria to achieve success in my role. During my 10 year career in social services, I built relationships with clients, medical teams, and government and private agencies to improve the quality of life of the clients I supported.

Recognized as someone skillful in persuading others to my point of view, I quickly gained the trust and respect of my clients and colleagues and the green light to implement innovative solutions and programming for the agencies I partnered with. I came to realize that these are life skills and I continued to leverage my reputation as an effective communicator and strong leader to help benefit the local organizations I volunteered for while later raising my children full-time.

3.  **Minimize the use of the word "I."** Vary your sentences to keep the reader engaged. Keep the writing style fluid and develop a tone that is somewhat conversational and develops rapport with the reader.

> Delivering exceptional customer service for financial services firms is what I do best. Over a 10 year career managing equities and fixed income transactions, I have consistently found ways to maximize client retention and P&L revenue through superior customer service. My experience spans four top-tier companies; Merrill Lynch, Morgan Stanley, UBS, and Lehman Brothers.

> Over the past 10 years, I have developed curriculum for and taught Basic Math, Pre-Algebra Developmental Reading, Basic College Reading, Paragraph and Essay Writing, and Spelling and Vocabulary to close to 1,000 students at Babat Junior College. I have consistently managed the needs of a broad range of learning, physical, sensory, and psychologically challenged students in large classroom settings. My classes are exceptionally diverse; not only from a disability perspective, but from an age, academic, socioeconomic, and cultural perspective as well.

4.  **Ask for the interview.** Create a strong call to action in your letter by expressing your interest in the company and requesting an in-person interview. Reiterate your reasons for feeling confident that you are the right match for the position.

> At this juncture, I am confidentially exploring new opportunities within the recording industry. An avid fan of hip-hop music, I believe my affinity for the music coupled with my extensive industry knowledge make me an excellent prospect for your organization. I am confident that I can deliver results similar to those described above for your label and look forward to a personal interview.

> For quite some time I have been impressed with your organization's mission and the advocacy work you have done and I would welcome the chance to meet with you to discuss my qualifications in more detail.

Excited by the prospect of an opportunity with your company and impressed by the strength of your brand, I would welcome the chance to meet with you to discuss my qualifications in more detail and look forward to a personal interview.

5. **Match your qualifications to the requirements of the job.** Create a cover letter that addresses each job requirement point by point. The stronger the match you can make between the two, the greater the likelihood of securing an interview. If the job description lists five core requirements and you are only proficient in two of them, the fit is not strong and it may not be an appropriate position for you to apply to. If the position description lists five requirements and you can speak to four or more of those requirements, the position is probably a good match.

## Your Selection Criteria

Demonstrated high-level research, analytical, oral and written communication skills; Experience preparing intelligence reports and delivering briefings.

## My Value Added

- Uncovered over $300M in fraudulent banking transactions and all related financial documentation in conjunction with investigative role for the United Nations Independent Inquiry. Documented findings for Committee's reports on program infractions to UN Security Council.

- Identified multimillion-dollar tax scam and money laundering scheme for Interpol.

## Your Selection Criteria

A high working knowledge of tactical and strategic intelligence and the ability to apply intelligence concepts. High level of ability to use computerized information management systems.

## My Value Added

- Contributed geopolitical and socioeconomic knowledge of Latin American business practices and culture to expose illicit business activity and maximize efficiency of evidence collection for Independent Inquiry Committee. Leveraged experience data mining financial/business news Web sites to "connect the dots" concerning Latin American affiliations and uncover improprieties.

- Trimmed time spent responding to police inquiries and improved data integrity significantly for Interpol by sourcing alternative methods for collecting and analyzing database information.

6. **Build rapport with your audience.** Discuss relevant business issues and ask thought-provoking questions to show your reader that you recognize their needs. Offer strategic solutions that position you as a thought leader who can add immediate value to the organization.

---

Re: President, Mercer College

The higher education needs of students, parents, and employers have changed dramatically over the past decade. For over 10 years, as a higher education senior administrator at Brookdale University and Bergen College, I have embraced change and introduced creative and more flexible curriculums that cater to the needs of the twenty-first century student. My passion for education and my expertise in analyzing processes and people have contributed to my successes in program development, curriculum redesign, blended, virtual, and experiential learning, and administrative process reengineering.

---

7. **Consider Including a famous quote to make your point.** Incorporating quotes that are relevant to the topics your letter is discussing is a great way to create a memorable letter that connects you to your reader. Quotes on efficiency, innovation, business development, and leadership can add a unique spin to your letter, a compelling value proposition, or a good conversation starter during an interview.

*"If your actions inspire others to dream more, learn more, do more and become more, you are a leader."* – John Quincy Adams

Dear Mr. Arnold:

Developing leaders to be the best they can be so they can inspire others is both my expertise and my passion. Whether I'm affecting change in a Fortune 500 company, cross-functional team, or individual, I strive to create opportunities for people to stretch that translate into increased ROI, improved productivity, and a more mission-driven corporate culture.

---

Dear Ms. Lewis:

*"I can't understand why people are frightened of new ideas. I'm frightened of old ones."* – John Cage

Consumer multi-media and wireless technologies are my expertise and my passion. Since the inception of digital imaging technology, I have been recognized as a thought leader, innovator, and spokesperson for the industry's most exciting products including mobile cameras and the PC cam. With a dual background in technology products marketing and electrical engineering, I bring instant credibility to any technology marketing team. Over the past 7 years, I have cultivated lucrative relationships with more than a dozen tier-one handset manufacturers, telecom service providers, application processor suppliers, and camera manufacturers to deliver phenomenal growth for Photag Technology.

---

Dear Mr. Leinweber:

*"The only way to know how customers see your business is to look at it through their eyes."* Daniel R. Scroggin, CEO

Putting myself in my customer's shoes when selling financial institutional research and product solutions has always come naturally to me. As a former institutional sales trader with 12 years of experience at leading firms including UBS, Merrill Lynch, and Mayner Securities, I have a keen sense of what tools will help traders make the best decisions for their firm and the customers they support.

8. **Keep the letter to one page.** Keep your cover letters short and use short paragraphs and bulleted lists to keep the reader's attention and make it easy for them to determine the match between your qualifications and their open job.

9. **Address the hiring authority by name.** The likelihood of building rapport with the reader and validating your interest in the job is increased when the inside cover address refers to the specific person rather than "Dear Sir." Whenever possible, sleuth around for additional information on the hiring manager so you can personalize your letter. Try surfing the company Web site to find the appropriate name or call the company directly to make an inquiry.

10. **Reference the position you are applying for.** Be sure to mention the job title and job number in the body of your letter as well as in your email subject line. Many hiring authorities request this information and your inability to follow their instructions could jeopardize your candidacy and lead them to believe that you have not paid attention to the details of their request.

11. **Sign your name.** Sounds obvious, but sometimes people overlook this detail. If you are sending a letter regular mail, include your handwritten signature. If your correspondence is via email, create an electronic signature.

# 9 Conclusion

Resumes are an important part of your job search strategy. The main focus of the resume is to get the interview and the information presented on the resume needs to be as compelling as possible in order to garner the attention of the hiring manager. By communicating your stories of success and integrating accomplishment-focused, metrics-driven information into the document, you quickly elevate your candidacy and increase the likelihood of gaining the attention of the hiring authority.

But a strong resume is just one part of your overall search strategy. Once you have crafted the perfect document, you need to make sure you are optimizing its presentation. Many job seekers turn to the job boards assuming that posting the resume online is the best method of search. The reality is exactly the opposite. While there are many jobs posted on the boards, numerous studies have indicated that only a tiny percentage (between 2% and 10%) of job seekers who use the boards find their jobs using this method. The job boards are noisy, crowded places. You may see a position that looks like it was custom made for you, but the reality is that there are probably at least another 100 applicants who think the same thing. Since there is rarely an existing relationship between the job seeker and the hiring authority in this scenario, it's hard to get picked out of the pile of applicants.

An additional 10%–20% of job seekers find their jobs through recruiters. A recruiter can be a great ally during a job search, but job seekers should keep in mind that when they are working with a recruiter, they are only exposing themselves to a certain percentage of the market...those companies that are willing to pay a recruiter to fill their open positions. In addition, recruiters are generally only going to be interested in your candidacy if your skill set matches a position in the recruiter's current job requisition portfolio. If your career path is not exceptionally linear you may not be the best client for a recruiter. Career changers, people returning to work, and people who have held several jobs in a relatively short period of time generally do not fare well with recruiters and people in these situations need to consider alternative methods of search.

Close to 70%–80% of people in search get their jobs through networking...the art of exchanging information continuously and graciously with members of their professional and social communities. People are more likely to share information with people they know and trust. So sharing information about job leads comes naturally in networking circles. Attempt to give more than you get and don't keep tabs on your goodwill versus someone else's and eventually you will find that you can almost always find a connection for whatever you need...whether it's an introduction to a business partner, advice on a project, or a tip on a job lead. Yes, this method is a lot of work, but it is quite rewarding to help others and receive their help in return.

Writing a resume requires introspection, objectivity, time, and good writing skills. Don't expect to create a powerful resume in an hour. And once you have completed your resume don't consider it finished. A resume is an evolving document and it is in your best interest to continue to review, scrutinize, and update the information you are presenting.

Once you land your new job, don't let your resume gather electronic dust in a file you never access. Each time you complete a project, jot a few notes to yourself about the impact of the project. Use the C-A-R strategy to craft your stories and keep these stories in a master file. Not only is this a great way to keep your resume up to date, but it's an excellent strategy for preparing for an annual performance review as well. By presenting your stories of success to your supervisor and quantifying how you have helped the company make money, save money, save time, grow the business, or keep the business, you improve your chances for making a business case for a higher merit increase or promotion.

Now that you have read this book and completed this first critical step to building a resume, you are well on your way to becoming "Happy About Your Resume."
I wish you success in your job search and beyond.

# Resume and Cover Letter Contributors

The following professional resume writers have contributed samples of their work to this book. Many have earned one or more of the following distinguishing professional credentials:

| | |
|---|---|
| CARW | Certified Advanced Resume Writer |
| CCM | Credentialed Career Master |
| CCMC | Credentialed Career Management Coach |
| CECC | Certified Electronic Career Coach |
| CEIP | Certified Employment Interview Professional |
| CERW | Certified Expert Resume Writer |
| CFRW | Certified Federal Resume Writer |
| CHRP | Certified Human Resources Professional |
| CJST | Certified Job Search Trainer |
| CPBA | Certified Professional Behavioral Analyst |
| CPBS | Certified Personal Branding Specialist |
| CPC | Certified Personnel Consultant |
| CPRW | Certified Professional Resume Writer |
| CRS | Certified Resume Strategist |
| CWDP | Certified Workforce Development Professional |
| FWCC | Federal Resume Writer Career Coach |
| IJCTC | International Job & Career Transition Coach |
| MCDP | Master Career Development Professional |
| MCRS | Master Certified Resume Strategist |
| MRW | Master Resume Writer |
| NCC | Nationally Certified Counselor |
| NCRW | Nationally Certified Resume Writer |
| VAL | Certified Values Arrangement List Administrator |

# Contributors

Jennifer Anthony
Resume ASAP
Portland, OR
888-295-4985
http://resumeasap.com
resumeasap@gmail.com

Wendy Belancourt, CPRW
Trend Resumes
St. Louis, Missouri
636-390-8580
wendy@trendresumes.com
http://trendresumes.com

Norine T. Dagliano, NCRW, CPRW, CFRW/CC
ekm Inspirations
Hagerstown, MD
301-766-2032
norine@ekminspirations.com
http://ekminspirations.com

Linda Dobogai, MS, MCDP, CPRW
Aberlene Resume & Career Services LLC
North Berlin, WI
414-425-6375
linda@aberleneresume.com
http://aberleneresume.com

Tamara Dowling, CPRW
Seeking Success
Valencia, CA
661-263-8709
TD@seekingsuccess.com
http://SeekingSuccess.com

Susan Easton, CRS, BFA
Competitive Edge Career Services
Prince George, BC
250-964-1138    Toll Free: 1-888-964-1138
NewCareer@cecs.ca
http://cecs.ca

Robyn L. Feldberg, CCMC, NCRW, VAL
Abundant Success Career Services
Frisco, TX
972-464-1144    Toll Free: (866) WIN-AJOB (1-866-946-2562)
Robyn@AbundantSuccessCareerServices.com
http://AbundantSuccessCareerServices.com

Cliff Flamer, MS, NCC, NCRW, CPRW
BrightSide Résumés
San Francisco/Bay Area, CA
Toll Free: 877-668-9767
writers@brightsideresumes.com
http://brightsideresumes.com

Wendy Gelberg, M.Ed., CPRW, IJCTC, CEIP
Gentle Job Search/Advantage Resumes
Needham, MA
781-444-0778
WGelberg@aol.com
http://gentlejobsearch.com

Meg Guiseppi, MRW, CPRW
Executive Resume Branding
Andover, NJ
973-726-0757
meg@ExecutiveResumeBranding.com
http://ExecutiveResumeBranding.com

Laura M. Labovich, MLRHR, CCM, CARW
A & E Consulting, LLC
Potomac Fall, VA
703-942-9390
lauramichelle@gmail.com
http://aspire-empower.com

Abby Locke, NCRW, MRW, CPBS
Premier Writing Services
Washington, DC
202-635-2197
alocke@premierwriting.com
http://premierwriting.com

John M. O'Connor, BA, MFA, CRW, CPRW, CCM, CECC, CFRW
Career Pro of NC, Inc.
Raleigh, NC
919-787-2400
john@careerproinc.com
http://careerproinc.com

Kris Plantrich, CPRW, CEIP
ResumeWonders
Ortonville, MI
248-627-2624    Toll Free: 888-789-2081
kris@resumewonders.com
http://resumewonders.com

Jared Redick
The Resume Studio
San Francisco, CA
415-846-6640
info@theresumestudio.com
http://theresumestudio.com

Jane Roqueplot, CPBA, CWDP, CECC
JaneCo's Sensible Solutions
Sharon, PA
724-342-0100    Toll Free: 1-888-JaneCos (526-3267)
Jane@janecos.com
http://janecos.com

Barbara Safani, MA, CERW, NCRW, CPRW, CCM
Career Solvers
New York, NY
212-579-7230    Toll Free: 866-333-1800
info@careersolvers.com
http://careersolvers.com

Kimberly Schneiderman, NCRW, CEIC
City Career Services
New York, NY
917-584-3022
kimberly@citycareerservices.com
http://citycareerservices.com

Tanya Taylor, CHRP, MCRS
TNT Human Resources Management
Brampton, ON
416-887-5819
Info@tntresumewriter.com
http://tntresumewriter.com

Claudine Vainrub, MBA, CPRW, CPBS, CPC
EduPlan, LLC
Aventura, FL
888-661-8234 / 786-547-9339
info@eduplan.us
http://eduplan.us

Ilona Vanderwoude, MRW, CCMC, CPRW, CJST, CEIP
Career Branches
New York, NY
718-971-6356
ilona@CareerBranches.com
http://CareerBranches.com

Rosa E. Vargas, NCRW, MRW
Creating Prints
407-802-4962
rvargas@creatingprints.com
http://creatingprints.com

Paul Willis, BA, CECC
Career Pro of NC, Inc.
Raleigh, NC
919-787-2400
paul@careerproinc.com
http://careerproinc.com

# Appendix B: Resume Samples

The following fictionalized resumes submitted by the professional resume writers listed in Appendix A epitomize the resume writing tips that have been discussed in the previous chapters. These samples are excellent examples of resumes that are not simply lists of tasks, but rather powerful marketing tools. Each one leverages strong accomplishment statements, professional competencies, powerful action verbs, and strategic design formats to quickly deliver a compelling message of the candidate's value to the hiring authority. This appendix covers sample resumes for professionals at every career stage from entry-level to C-suite executive in a variety of fields including finance, marketing, technology, operations, manufacturing, sales, construction management, healthcare, and education.

**Jennifer Anthony**
Sample: *John Jobseeker*

**Wendy Belancourt, CPRW**
Sample: *Peter Clements*

**Norine T. Dagliano, NCRW, CPRW, CFRW/CC**
Samples: *Jennifer Dutchison, Stephen Fu, Mason Turner, Denton Chambers*

**Linda Dobogai, MS, MCDP, CPRW**
Samples: *Laura Sykes, Ellen Carlson*

**Tamara Dowling, CPRW**
Sample: *Laura Solon*

**Susan Easton, CRS, BFA**
Sample: *Michelle Hiscock*

**Robyn L. Feldberg, CCMC, NCRW, VAL**
Samples: *John Taylor Spain, Melissa Edwards, Christopher Johnson*

**Cliff Flamer, MS, NCC, NCRW, CPRW**
Samples: *Jon Lugent, Willa Sandy Merrick*

**Wendy Gelberg, M.Ed., CPRW, IJCTC, CEIP**
Sample: *Michael Delgado*

**Meg Guiseppi, MRW, CPRW**
Samples: *Mark S. Paladino, Yolanda Rodriguez*

**Laura M. Labovich, MLRHR, CCM, CARW**
Sample: *Lee Smith*

**Abby Locke, NCRW, MRW, CPBS**
Samples: *Audrey MacDonald, Jerry Zimmer*

**John M. O'Connor, BA, MFA, CRW, CPRW, CCM, CECC, CFRW**
Sample: *Christy R. Reyes*

**Kris Plantrich, CPRW, CEIP**
Sample: *Sissy Commons*

**Jared Redick**
Samples: *Jay Wiley, Nanette Holt, Cynthia Kato, Madison Cowell*

**Jane Roqueplot, CPBA, CWDP, CECC**
Samples: *Melanie Simmons, Mary Sharper, Carol Grande*

**Barbara Safani, MA, CERW, NCRW, CPRW, CCM**
Samples: *Barry Morgan, Rebecca Small*

**Kimberly Schneiderman, NCRW, CEIC**
Sample: *Michael Sugar*

**Tanya Taylor, CHRP, MCRS**
Samples: *Shirley Edwards, Stan Wilson*

**Claudine Vainrub, MBA, CPRW, CPBS, CPC**
Sample: *Kelly Lowe*

**Ilona Vanderwoude, MRW, CCMC, CPRW, CJST, CEIP**
Sample: *David P. Johnson*

**Rosa E. Vargas, NCRW, MRW**
Samples: *Thomas Strong, Erica Sweeney*

**Paul Willis, BA, CECC**
Sample: *Christy R. Reyes*

# ELLEN S. CARLSON

■ *822 North 12<sup>th</sup> Street* ■ *Burlington, Wisconsin 53454* ■ *414-555-5232* ■ *ecarl@sbcglobal.com*

## ACCOUNT MANAGEMENT - PROFILE

*Medical Device Sales ~ Customer Relationship Management ~ Revenue-Growth Orientation*

High-energy, tenacious professional with proven ability to achieve high sales volume. Established a new record at Vascular Solutions for the highest quarterly sales ever in my assigned territory; increased market share; fast-track promoted. Dynamic relationship influencer who effectively uses medical background and "insider" understanding of hospital bureaucracies to establish credibility, reach decision-makers, and close sales. Numerous call point relationships include cardiologists, interventional radiologists, vascular surgeons, department directors, RNs, technicians, and purchasing agents.

### Areas of Expertise:

| | | |
|---|---|---|
| ✓ B2B Direct Sales | ✓ Customer Satisfaction | ✓ Customer Retention / Loyalty |
| ✓ Clinical Knowledge | ✓ Increased Volume | ✓ Product Launch |
| ✓ Competitive Positioning | ✓ Strategic Planning | ✓ Sales Management |
| ✓ Presentations / Closings | ✓ Cold Calling | ✓ Customer Needs Assessment |

## PROFESSIONAL EXPERIENCE

**OMSBED CORPORATION** - Burlington, Wisconsin                      May 2007 – Present
*Multi-national corporation developing and selling vascular devices; $45 million net revenue in 2007.*
### Account Manager

Use consultative sales approach to sell cardiac cath lab, electrophysiology, and interventional radiology devices to hospitals as sole representative in territory that covers the entire State of Wisconsin. Grow existing accounts and develop new client relationships. Key accounts include *Froedtert Hospital, Aurora Health Care, University of Wisconsin, Dean Health System, Columbia-St. Mary's,* and *Children's Hospital.* Introduce new products to the market. Create / enhance marketing documents, customizing according to customer needs.

### Sales Accomplishments:
- Named "Midwest Account Rep of the Quarter" in April 2008 for largest increase of overall sales across the region.
- Promoted from Associate Account Manager position soon after hired due to stellar sales performance – achieved 138.5% to plan for first quarter quota and >100% to plan all subsequent quarters.
- Catapulted from total sales ranking of 51<sup>st</sup> out of 66 sales reps to 7<sup>th</sup> out of 68 nationally within a year after being hired.
- Virtually doubled quarterly sales within six months; won clients over by using medical expertise to provide group in-services (for up to 40 hospital personnel at a time) and individualized trainings to demonstrate product value.
- Successfully negotiated significant one-item contract for $53,500.

### Account Development / Product Introduction Achievements:
- Grew active customer base by 50% in less than a year by effectively leveraging relationships to develop new accounts and by successfully introducing innovative products.
- Consistently named in the top 20 (often top 10) sales reps throughout the company.

**CAPITAL EMERGENCY PHYSICIANS**
**ALL SAINTS HEALTH CARE** - Burlington, Wisconsin                July 2004 – May 2007
### Physician Assistant – Emergency Department

Obtain patient H & Ps; provide medical treatment for diseases, illnesses, and pain; perform various medical procedures; order and interpret lab and diagnostic tests; and administer discharge medications, instructions, follow up care, and / or hospital admission.

**74**                                **Appendix B: Resume and Cover Letter Samples**

EMERGENCY MEDICAL ASSOCIATES
BURLINGTON MEMORIAL HOSPITAL - Burlington, Wisconsin          March 2002 – June 2004
**Physician Assistant – Emergency Department**

Assessed and treated patients requiring emergency care.

ERGI-MED, S.C.
ST. JOHN'S MEDICAL CENTER - Milwaukee, Wisconsin             Feb1999 – Dec 2001
**Physician Assistant – Emergency Department**

Assessed and treated patients requiring emergency care.

MIDWEST HEART INSTITUTE
ST. JOHN'S MEDICAL CENTER - Milwaukee, Wisconsin             May 1997 – Jan 1999
**Physician Assistant – Cardiovascular Surgery**

Assisted with and / or performed various cardiovascular surgical procedures including EVH for CABG, valve replacements, heart & lung transplants, and thoracotomies.

GUTHRIE MEDICAL SERVICES - Burlington, Wisconsin            May 1995 – May 1997
**Registered Nurse – ICU and Emergency Departments**

Provided skilled nursing care to patients in the CVICU, ICU, and Emergency Room in various hospitals throughout the Milwaukee area.

CARDIOVASCULAR ICU
ST. JOHN'S MEDICAL CENTER - Milwaukee, Wisconsin            June 1994 – May 1995
**Registered Nurse – CVICU**

Provided skilled nursing care for post-operative patients.

MCCAIN PHARMACEUTICALS, INC. - Madison, Wisconsin           Jan – May 1994
**Pharmaceutical Sales Representative**

Promoted medications to hospitals and clinics in the Madison area. Educated healthcare personnel on use, side effects, dosing guidelines, and drug interactions of various pharmaceuticals. Met all sales quotas. Top graduate in training class of 200 reps.

## EDUCATION

UNIVERSITY OF WISCONSIN - Madison, Wisconsin

**Bachelor of Science – Physician Assistant**, 1997
~ Graduated with Honors; GPA 3.7 / 4.0

**Bachelor of Science – Nursing**, 1994
~ Graduated with Honors; GPA 3.7 / 4.0

## CERTIFICATIONS & AFFILIATIONS

National Commission on Certification of Physician Assistants: PA-C #1057555
Physician Assistant Wisconsin License #1559 – 023; Registered Nurse Wisconsin License #134943-055
ACLS & BLS Certified
Member of Society of Emergency Medicine Physician Assistants
Member of American Academy of Physician Assistants

# Denton J. Chambers

82 Foxleigh Lane • Tampa, FL 33601
352.555.5004 • dchambers@gmail.com

## Sales Profile

Ambitious and self-disciplined professional with more than 20 years of $B_2B$ sales experience solidifying customer relations, enhancing brand image, and maintaining competitive advantage for key players in the retail and wholesale apparel industry. A natural born sales professional with talent for generating enthusiasm, instilling confidence, and influencing change to ensure highest levels of productivity while consistently generating revenue gains. Creative problem solving, a positive sense of humor, and excellent verbal skills have been the framework for accomplishing goals through people.

*"I believe if a new system, tool, or technology emerges within a business, it is up to the employees to make it work."*

*Sales competencies include*
Brand Management
Account Revitalization
Business Optimization
Market Trends
Product Upgrades
Key Account Management
Product Demonstrations
Inventory Control
Team Development

## Career Highlights & Achievements

*A unique blend of interpersonal and computer technology skills have been the cornerstones of sustained achievement in improving operations and increasing market share for Aquamor America.*

| | |
|---|---|
| **Sales & Merchandising:** | • Consistently has achieved annual sales increases – grew four-state territory from $800K to over $11M annual sales volume. |
| | • Annually produce 20% of Aquamor's $40M team-sales revenues while managing only 10% of accounts. |
| | • Took key account from $1.5M to $3.3M by injecting product knowledge and reenergizing marketing strategies. |
| | • Cornered 80% of prime merchandising floor-plan and ignited 20% sales increase for three specialty retailers. |
| | • Received numerous awards for extraordinary sales performance. |
| **Computer Technology:** | • Played instrumental role in steering company-wide implementation of SAP |
| | • Converted technology-resistant national sales team into competent end-users. |
| | • Created all variances to produce customized sales reports. |
| | • Developed sales force to support e-commerce business operations. |
| | • Pioneered initial e-mail broadcasts to dealers. |
| | • Recognized as *SAP Super User,* granted three special recognition awards. |

## Professional Experience

**Aquamor America, *a Division of Pinellas Swimwear, Inc.*—**1988 to Present
**Sales Associate/Senior Account Representative**

Working from Tampa, FL home-based office, develop and manage multiple distribution channels to drive sales for company's Retail Sales Division (department stores, specialty and sports-equipment retailers, military) and Team Sales Division (dealers specializing in outfitting c and college swim teams).

Generate $11M+ annual sales across four-state territory encompassing FL, AL, MS and eastern GA. Manage 30 team-accounts, and numerous specialty accounts.

Supervise two field sales representative and one administrative assistant.

*Continued...*

**Sales Associate/Senior Account Representative** *(continued)*

**Evaluate competitive market trends and implement sales and operational strategies to ensure long-term and sustainable growth.**
*Proof:*

- Revitalized a lagging account, help them recover from bankruptcy, and generated positive cash flow by realigning distribution channel to enhance competitive product positioning.

- Championed and led total remodeling and remerchandising of three specialty stores; transformed each to successful retail operation, cornered 80% of prime merchandising floor-plan, and produced 20% increase in retail sales.

- Influenced Naval Air Station Key West's and Navy Exchange's decision to adopt Aquamor as part of the official recruit training uniform and created stimulus for implementing auto-replenishment for basic merchandise.

- Created new revenue stream ($150K annually) by overcoming Navy Exchange's long-standing resistance to expanding available product line to include goggles and accessories.

- Converted $100K Navy Exchange account to $750K account over three years.

- Shed light on disconnect between sales and production and pushed through change that corrected inaccurate readings of Work-in-progress (WIP) vs. on-hand inventory and enhanced order fulfillment and distribution process.

- Assisted National Team Sales Manager in developing programs to drive nationwide sales initiatives.

**Demonstrate leadership as knowledgeable computer technology resource, creative problem solver, and "go-to guy" for company's sales force.**
*Proof:*

- Tagged by senior management for eight-person SAP implementation team to provide leadership and direction to national sales force throughout pilot testing and system integration.

- Overcame sales team's technology resistance by enthusiastically endorsing system capabilities and providing step-by-step guidance to conquer individual learning curves.

- Identified tracking and reporting requirements and personally developed all variances to produce customized sales reports.

- Consulted with customer service in creating and delivering SAP end-user webinars for national sales representatives.

- Serve as liaison between sales and MIS team regarding system modifications to improve operations.

**Prior Experience:** Established broad scope of buying, merchandising, inventory control, sales, and retail management experience with department stores that turned multimillion-dollar annual sales: Sales Associate, *Fine Menswear Company*; Assistant Buyer, *Wayne & Winthrop*; and Assistant/Group Manager, *The Highton Company*.

# PETER CLEMENTS
## SENIOR MARKETING EXECUTIVE
*Drives exceptional market performance and delivers benchmark growth.*

**Professional integrity, a big-picture focus, and history of driving significant gains in profitability** are the cornerstones of a career distinguished by sustained accomplishments with a "blue-chip" marketing pedigree (MasterCard, American Lending). Respected as intuitive start-up and turnaround strategist, and record-breaking implementation leader. Full spectrum marketing programs across LAC international channels leveraging strategic alliances. High ROI contributor to companies seeking expertise in data management-driven programs that deepen customer brand loyalty and dramatically increase profitability. Fluent in English, Spanish, and Portuguese.

- **Repeated success driving multimillion-dollar sales increases, unprecedented customer loyalty, and brand differentiation through "high-octane", growth-enabling marketing strategies and campaigns.**
- **P&L "maximizer," with history of doubling consumer response while concurrently reducing marketing spends.**
- **Respected leader of diverse creative teams; innovator of programs/collateral proven to outdistance the competition; strategist, key resource, and problem-solver for senior executive colleagues.**

### EXPERTISE

| | |
|---|---|
| ◆ Strategic & Tactical Marketing | ◆ Brand, Message & Image Development |
| ◆ $8MM P&L Management | ◆ Customer Acquisition, Loyalty & Retention |
| ◆ Staff Leadership | ◆ Product Strategy, Development & Launch |
| ◆ Cross-Functional Collaboration | ◆ Strategic Alliance & Partnership Management |
| ◆ Campaign & Turnkey Project Management | ◆ Decision Support & Knowledge Management |
| ◆ End-to-End Process Management | ◆ Integrated & Cross-Channel Marketing |

## CAREER HIGHLIGHTS

**QUARTERBACKED "BUSINESS REWARDS" MERCHANT PROGRAM FOR MASTERCARD.**
Conceptualized and implemented a strategic initiative maximizing P&L of companies $2^{nd}$ largest financial expense. Pioneered innovative decision support system empowering fee structure optimization across all markets. Created and aggressively negotiated well-received redemption programs.

**PROGRAM RESULTS**
- **Over 600% ROI.**
- **40% incremental revenue, $1M $1^{st}$ year.**
- **$2M+ annual liability cost reduction.**

**RECIPIENT OF 2002 MASTERCARD CHAIRMAN'S AWARD FOR QUALITY**
- Latin American leader in development and implementation of CLOUD platform, a 2-year, $6M redemption system initiative. Implemented with a cross functional team of 75+ across technology, operations, finance, and marketing. Led first pilot rollouts into region then advised on EMEA and JAPA segments.

Pioneered customer behavioral modeling and predictability software platform based on profitability, usage, tenure, and product type.

Rolled out throughout Latin America and orchestrated training of 1,200 Customer Service Representatives.

**IGNITED LAC REGIONAL SALES TO $20M PROJECTED NPV ON ROI VIA CROSS-SELL PROGRAM INITIATIVE.**

**Led major initiative encompassing complex spectrum of American Lending products and programs.**

753 SW 8<sup></sup>th Street ◆ Provost, UT 26897 ◆ 264-390-1375 ◆ pclements@yahoo.com

Appendix B: Resume and Cover Letter Samples

# EXECUTIVE PERFORMANCE

MARKETING COMMUNICATIONS COMPANY
*Full-service advertising and direct marketing boutique acency for U.S. Hispanic and Latin American markets.*

### PARTNER – DM & CLIENT SERVICES HEAD | 2004 – PRESENT

Holds direct accountability for strategic vision, conceptualization, feasibility, development, deployment, and support of client marketing initiatives across several industries. Manages touch points through first-year engagements, targeting cross-sell, retention, frequency marketing, anti-attrition, and SAC programs.

◆ Won and spearheaded $3M American Lending project delivering an end-to-end U.S. Hispanic market development and implementation initiative. Aligned brand to culture and devised above the line / below the line (ATL / BTL) launch campaign programs. Seamlessy orchestrated via cross-matrixed collaboration with agency staff, executive leaders, 15 client divisions, and external client partners.

◆ Conceptualized and rolled out bi-lingual (Spanish and Portuguese) SAP Latin America's B2B online and classical media campaigns into 15 SME markets driving 45% incremental sales over previous campaigns.

MARKETING COMMUNICATIONS COMPANY
*Start-up consultancy providing loyalty and rewards marketing strategy.*

### PARTNER – VICE PRESIDENT | 2002 – 2004

Envisioned and implemented key strategies optimizing clients' profitability by employing loyalty strategies, programs, and service enhancements.

◆ Won and managed 11 international contracts valued up to $100K with MasterCard Latin America, International Trust Bank Sri Lanka, National Bank of Peru, People's Bank of Puerto Rico, Bank of Chile, Credit Union of Central America, Interbank, and the Bank of Colombia.

MASTERCARD
*Fortune 500 Credit Card Company.*

### LATIN AMERICA & CARIBBEAN REGIONAL HEAD – CUSTOMER LOYALTY | 2001 – 2002
### LATIN AMERICA & CARIBBEAN REGIONAL HEAD – MEMBERSHIP REWARDS | 1997 – 2001

Chosen from select "invitation only" group of top performers to oversee LAC region following record-breaking program roll-out success in Brazil. Challenged to take program to next level of profitability. Held direct $8M P&L and regional investment responsibility. Directed a cross-country staff of 10. Managed $5M annual budget. Led key cross-functional teams in $MM projects.

Repositioned to larger loyalty program oversight following 2001 re-organization. Managed end-to-end customer life cycle ensuring consumer satisfaction and profitability through new customer activation, cross-sell, frequency programs, behavioral modeling, usage promotions, enrollment services, up-sell, and customer retention programs.

◆ Created "Merchants Plus Program", a revenue-generating point sales product generating 500% ROI. Designed infrastructure with incremental sales tracking tool, the defining success factor for high-volume merchant acceptance.

◆ Reduced redemption liability costs approximately $1M annually through widely-accepted raffle program reducing yearly point spends by 150M.

◆ Developed strategic alliances with Varit, TEM, Mexicana, LanChile, Hertz, Hilton, Marriott, and Starwood, enhancing value proposition and increasing consumer spend $3.6M yearly.

◆ Partnered with Ogilvy & Mather to manage brand. Rolled out annual regional and global campaigns delivering up to 85% program enrollment.

---

753 SW 8ᵗʰ Street ◆ Provost, UT 26897 ◆ 264-390-1375 ◆ pclements@yahoo.com

## EXECUTIVE PERFORMANCE

MASTERCARD CONTINUED...

MANAGER – MEMBERSHIP REWARDS PROGRAM | SÃO PAULO – BRAZIL | 1994 – 1997 | **Developed and directed Brazil's first Membership Rewards program.** Managed branding, collateral, and product positioning, directing a staff of 7. Designed MIS to effectively track programs success. **Generated 25% first-year incremental spending increase, a company record.**

MANAGER – CARD ACQUISITION / DIRECT MARKETING | SÃO PAULO – BRAZIL | 1991 – 1994 | Managed solo mailings, supplementary card stuffers, member lead, and member-get-member card acquisition campaigns. **Increased net response rate 40%** utilizing segmentation techniques, database management, channel mix, creative direct mail package, and offer testing strategies.

~ Began career with MasterCard as college intern within direct mail division; promoted twice to Coordinator and Manager respectively. ~

---

## EDUCATION

### BACHELOR OF SOCIAL COMMUNICATIONS & MARKETING
UNIVERSITY OF MARKETING | São Paulo, Brazil

### DIRECT MARKETING CERTIFICATE
NEW STATE UNIVERSITY

PROFESSIONAL DEVELOPMENT

Train the Trainers/Membership Rewards Program | Frequency Marketing Inc.
Striking a Balance, A Risk Management Course | MasterCard
Beyond the Basics – Direct Marketing | MasterCard
Best Practices in Interactive Marketing | MasterCard
Online Media | Ogilvy & Mather

---

## PROFESSIONAL AFFILIATIONS

- Direct Marketing Association **(DMA)**
- Association of Hispanic Advertising Agencies **(AHAA)**
- International Advertising Association **(IAA)**
- 2008 **Presenter** | Strategic Marketing Institutes 14th Annual Marketing Conference | *Presentation of technology in marketing to LAC markets.*

---

753 SW 8th Street • Provost, UT 26897 • 264-390-1375 • pclements@yahoo.com

# SISSY COMMONS

scommons@meadowlark.biz

1267 Domino Ct.
Spring, TX 77386

832.556.6678 (H)
832.807.1123 (C)

## IT SECURITY CONSULTANT

Remarkable 20 year career integrating outstanding experience and cutting-edge technology to deliver strategic global security solutions for medium and large sized companies and government agencies. Leverage adept leadership, negotiation and project management skills to maintain superior customer service while developing and deploying web reporting strategies and marketing the latest IT products and services.

> *"Sissy has equipped our hotels with advanced capabilities which allow access to other Bayley hotel reservations systems as well as authorization to set up blocks of rooms for conference related reservations. The changes Sissy implemented have decreased standing room vacancies by 6% in its first year. Great job." – Jim Farr, V.P. of Reservations, Bayley Hotels*

### CORE COMPETENCIES:

- ◆ Senior Quality Assurance Engineering
- ◆ Expert Presentation Experience
- ◆ Project Management
- ◆ Troubleshooting & Customer Support
- ◆ Security Advisor
- ◆ Team Building and Leadership
- ◆ Custom Software Engineering
- ◆ Network Administration

### TECHNICAL APPLICATIONS:

**Security:** Penetration Testing, Vulnerability Assessments, Firewall Policy, Incident Response and Firewall Activity reporting.

**Language and Software:** JAVA, HTML, ASP, PERL, CGI, Hyperion OLAP, ORACAL, SQL, Netscape server, IIS server, Apache server, Firewalls.

**Operation Systems:** Windows 2000 / XP / NT 4.0, LINUX, SUNOS, SPUX and BSD.

**Hardware:** CISCO Routers, BIG IP F5, INTEL, Solaris Cobalt, LINUX, VA LINUX, Wireless Networks and Firewalls

## CAREER HISTORY

**MEADOWLARK.BIZ,** Houston, TX        2002 to Present

**CTO/Security Consultant**

Formed this IT consulting firm from the ground up, pairing security related products with medium and large size companies such as PhotoLens, EXIT, and Bayley Hotels as well as different branches of government. Accountable for managing business operations, facilitating client development, and installation of several custom security configurations for national and international companies.

- ◆ Developed a web-based vulnerability assessment tool successfully utilized by numerous clients.
- ◆ Accomplished Technical Security Speaker of several security conferences nationwide.

*Continued...*

♦ Developed security solutions for Aspen Inc., and reconfigured the StarGear reservation reporting tool for Bayley Hotels.

♦ Authored and utilized custom reports and profiles to fit new Oracle Portal driven website for PhotoLens.

**BOZEMAN CORPORATION,** Waco, TX                                   1996 to 2002

**Senior Security Consultant** (2000 to 2002)

Promoted to senior project manager position overseeing major security accounts including TileMart, ADL, MRAA, and NewBank. Interfaced with upper management as advisor on security trends and roadmaps, specifically "Edge Prevention Detection Lab" with @risk and Microsoft. Advised on penetration testing, computer forensic and "Clown and Dancer" round tables.

♦ Developed several applications such as courseware for European security partners, and custom Wireless and VoIP security tests for Security Cover.

♦ Spoke at several technical security conferences including, TechSchool, TechMinds, and NetConference.

**Senior Professional Service Engineer** (1998 to 2000)

Advanced to senior project manager by delivering top-notch support to high-profile Web Triumph accounts. Managed several clients hosting 50 to 500 web servers.

♦ Sustained 100% success rate on all Firefly Suite engagements.

♦ Built custom Web Triumphs tools and implemented "TopHat Team", a strategic team of highly skills individuals that converge to resolve issues Tech Support can not.

♦ Generated web analytic field tools including tracking tools and SCRIBE scripts.

**Senior Quality Assurance Engineer** (1996 to 1998)

Brought onboard as senior quality assurance engineer accountable for designing, implementing and maintaining a quality assurance lab for Grantee Server, Security Cover and Firefly Suite. Provided design and implementation of Charge Lab and alpha and beta test programs for OS platforms of LINUX, UNIX, and Microsoft.

**ENVIRONNET.COM,** Pasadena, TX                                   1993 to 1996

**Network/Security Administrator**

Hired to oversee security of e-commerce sites and internal servers. Designed physical and technical security programs. Managed security audits, integrated intrusion detection and accessed control systems. Supervised and mentored new staff members and assisted management in writing procedures and department manual.

---

## EDUCATION

**Bachelor of Science Degree in Information Technology**
TEXAS A & M, College Station, TX

# MADISON COWELL

1234 Main Street, Seattle, WA 98101 | 206-123-4567 | info@theresumestudio.com

## Product Development / Experience Design Director

Social Software • eCommerce Platforms • Consumer Products

Technically sophisticated and business-savvy professional with over 18 years of experience building business solutions through product / project management and user experience design. Manage budgets up to $19 MM, and teams of up to 50 engineers, graphic designers, copy and technical writers, information architects, and vendors.

Collegial negotiator and trusted executive advisor, with expertise launching websites and applications. Combine qualitative user experience with quantitative analytics to build market-leading products.

Career highlights:

- Drove strategy, design and implementation of social networking site for people over 50 – **Boomertown.com**
- Directed launch team and site development for **FamousSite.com – ING Entertainment**
- Led New York-based development team for U.S. launch of Paris site – **StoreFront.net**
- Recognized by E*Trade's founder, Christos Cotsakos for "Excellence in Service."

## Experience

**VICE PRESIDENT, PRODUCT DEVELOPMENT** (9/06–present)
**DIRECTOR OF USER EXPERIENCE** (3/04–9/06)
Product Roadmap, Requirements & Design | Workflow | Feature Sets | Communication Facilitation

**Boomertown**, Seattle, WA
Recruited by founder as first hire to manage $1.2 MM alpha launch of new social networking site for people over 50. Partnered with Founder, CEO, and Chief Product Officer to shape vision from development to launch.

Hired original team of four user experience personnel, growing to 15 within 12 months. Integrated in-house team with brand design / strategy and technical engineering vendor teams. Managed 4 direct reports. Reported to Chief Product Officer.

- Launched site September 2006, after six-month development and 8-month alpha launch.
- Increased membership by 47% in Q1 08.
- Post alpha-launch product development highlights: Taxonomy to tag-based navigation system conversion; site template IA and look/feel redesign; Profile experience improvement; Content and Site Member findability improvements; Message Center build out; and SEO optimization.

**SENIOR DEVELOPMENT PROJECT MANAGER** (1/02–3/04)
Project Accountability | Timelines & Procedures | Product Cohesiveness

**StoreFront.net**, New York, NY
Key clients: Nike, Converse, Boston Market, and the New York Giants.

Recruited to 26-month contract, managing eCommerce platform rewrite. Developed practices and guidelines for project two years behind schedule. Charged with turning around six under-functioning divisions and building morale during system-wide rearchitecture of brittle code. Indirectly managed 45 personnel. Reported to SVP of Engineering.

- Launched re-coded eCommerce platform within projected 9-month on-time window.
- Increased productivity by over 60% across four functional areas.
- Retained 11 of 11 engineers during high personnel turnover period.
- Restored investor confidence, and fostered new client growth.

**Happy About My Resume** 83

## SENIOR PRODUCER (4/00–1/02)
Ethnographic Research | Project Budgets & Schedules | Design Reviews

**Hot Knife**, Boston, MA
Recruited to manage user experience and visual design on behalf of high visibility clients during period of rapid growth. Bid projects ranging from $10,000 to $350,000. Managed working sessions, card sorts, usability testing, stakeholder interviews and presentations, multi-round signoffs, and team productivity.

- Supervised user experience and visual redesign of **E*Trade.com**'s public customer site, teaming with 15 E*Trade decision-makers through three rounds of signoffs.
- Facilitated close of **WellsFargo.com** user experience redesign.
- Oversaw **Lord and Taylor** user experience redesign, integrating four siloed platforms used by 3,000 corporate and retail employees nationwide.
- Managed user experience redesign of sales tool used by 6,000 **Bank of America** Customer Service Representatives nationwide.

## PRODUCT & PROGRAM MANAGEMENT CONSULTANT (9/96–4/00)
Business Requirements Sets | Project Proposals, Tracking, Reporting & Evaluation | User Experience Design

**E*Trade Financial** (Headquarters), New York, NY
Recruited to cross-functional management positions in three business units and $19 MM budget. Established best practices and communication tools. Ensured stable implementation across multi-million user platforms. Managed vendors and teams of up to 40. Reported to Vice President of each business unit.

- **Investment Advice Division Project** (3/99 to 4/00): Standardized management protocols for group comprising nine product managers and 25 technologists.
  - Streamlined division processes across 23 projects.
  - Designed Rational Unified Process training for 40 employees.
- **Banking Division Product** (10/97 to 3/99): Managed ABC product rollout, a first-generation product combining checking and brokerage accounts at E*Trade.
  - Led requirements gathering workshops comprising nine business unit / 45-person nationwide team.
- **Brokerage Division Product** (9/96 to 10/97): Management of Portfolio and Market Alerts, sent daily to 1.5 million of E*Trade's highest net worth clients.

Early Internet startup career as Associate Producer, Senior Project Manager, and Program Manager in Silicon Valley, California; New York, New York; and Paris, France.

---

## Profile

---

### Education
B.A., *with distinction*
Columbia University, New York, NY

### Professional Development
The Project Management Institute
- PMP Certification, *1999*

### Volunteerism
The Food Bank of New York, *2002-present*

### Technology
Mac / Windows Environments: MS Office Suite, Adobe InDesign Suite, Omnigraffle, Confluence Jira, Pivotal Tracker, MS Project, Visio, Rational Tool Suite (RUP), Basecamp

1234 Main Street, Seattle, WA 98101 | 206-123-4567 | info@theresumestudio.com

# Michael Delgado

*Bringing balance and simplicity to Human Resources processes*

420 Evergreen St.
Wellesley, MA 02481

781-555-5555
mdelgado@abc.com

## PROFILE

**Human Resource Director** with MBA and experience in positions of progressive responsibility in all aspects of human resources. More than ten years of proven managerial skills. Background includes strategic leadership and executive coaching in international organizations. Strong track record driving management/staff collaboration to achieve business goals. Expert in compliance and HR practices in an FDA regulated environment. Excellent communication skills

## CAREER HIGHLIGHTS

**Training:** Developed and implemented original training and guides for delivering comprehensive and consistent content to advance the mission of the organization. Balanced the best interests of the organization with the needs of employees to achieve organizational goals. Implemented best management practices that increased employee engagement in multinational businesses.

**Staffing:** Identified and defined high quality candidates in a tight job market and reduced cost per hire and turnaround time in many diverse organizations. Managed succession planning and employee development programs to build for the future and retain top talent.

**Executive Coaching:** Coached senior management as a trusted advisor, to develop and communicate strategy for continuous improvement and organizational effectiveness.

**Organizational Development:** Integrated cross-functional teams to change corporate culture and define common vision of success. Drove change targeted at strategic growth.

**Benefits and Compensation:** Built infrastructure to support multi-tiered compensation in medical products industry. Implemented benefits and compensation programs in multiple industries to provide strong ROI.

**Labor Law:** Collaborated with legal team to establish policies and procedures in compliance with FDA regulations and fair labor practices. Trained management in legal hiring practices to ensure compliance during period of rapid growth.

## EXPERIENCE

MEDICAL SOLUTIONS, INC., Shrewsbury, MA                                   2006–present
**Director of Human Resources**
Provide a full spectrum of human resources support for medical device division. Manage all legal and compliance issues resulting in successful completion of a TUV audit; perform executive-level consulting in organizational development; coaching; results-oriented training, development and implementation; and strategic planning.

*Key Accomplishments:*
- Built partnerships among corporate functions such as Operations, IT, Quality, Finance, to achieve organizational effectiveness and promote collaboration across boundaries.
- Introduced effective human resources practices and management development forums that created an internal pipeline of management talent throughout the organization.
- Developed streamlined analytical tools to enhance HR decision-making by providing real-time data
- Established staffing practices that consistently attract and retain top talent and resulted in 15% higher scores on employee satisfaction survey.

## EXPERIENCE (continued)

GLOBAL MEDICAL SYSTEMS, Worcester, MA        2001–2006
**Worldwide Director of Human Resources**
Provided human resources support for worldwide patient monitoring division producing revenues approaching $1 billion. Drove strategic planning and management effectiveness that resulted in progressive higher employee engagement survey scores.

*Key Accomplishments:*
♦ Implemented a management and employee development program to enable the workforce to adapt to a highly competitive and increasingly demanding business climate.
♦ Reduced time-to-hire by 20% as a result of effective interviewing practices and accelerated decision-making.
♦ Built strong senior management team through 360-degree feedback and aggressive goal setting.

INFOTECH CORPORATION, Marlborough, MA (headquartered in Milpitas, CA)        1997–2001
**Sr. Human Resources Manager**
Reorganized the management structure for a bicoastal Engineering Division.

*Key Accomplishments:*
♦ Built strong partnership with the executive staff to ensure that managers and employees worked collaboratively to achieve business goals across two sites by implementing programs that drove high productivity and job satisfaction.
♦ Maximized staffing and compensation practices by basing hiring and pay programs on workforce plans, succession plans, and individual development plans. Program focused on job growth and employee development in order to train internal candidates to fill hard-to-staff positions.

DIGITAL EQUIPMENT CORPORATION, Maynard, MA        1983–1997
**Sr. Human Resources Manager** Worldwide Sales and Marketing Division Headquarters
Held positions of increasing scope and responsibility in various Digital departments.

*Key Accomplishments:*
♦ Oversaw the effective delivery of all human resources management, including compensation, recruitment, HR information systems, and university relations.
♦ Implemented an Alternative Dispute Resolution (ADR) program with anticipated savings of millions of dollars in litigation costs.
♦ **Awarded:** Digital Achievement Award for Outstanding Contributions to Diversity Work, Digital Achievement Award for Competitive Benchmarking, Managerial Excellence Award, and Educational Services Instructor Excellence Award.

Prior experience includes training and human resources positions at State Street Financial Services, General Mills, and Polaroid Corporation.

## EDUCATION

| | |
|---|---|
| **MBA** | Executive Program, Babson College, Babson Park, MA |
| **BA** | Communications, Speech and English, State University College of New York at Albany |
| **Certificate** | Mediation and Dispute Resolution, New England Mediation Services, Cambridge, MA |

# Rose Dollinger

*1045 Forest Road ◉ Abbottsford, BC V2N 2P7*
*Phone: (250) 456-7651 ◉ Email: rdollinger@allegro.com*

## Professional Web Designer

A talented and results-oriented professional, balancing creative and artistic skills with technical proficiency and a critical eye for details. Adaptable and collaborative, with remarkable problem-solving abilities and communication skills. Expertise includes an Associate Certificate in Web Technologies, over 6 years providing progressive web development and design to support client businesses, and key competencies in the following areas:

- ◉ Search engine optimization
- ◉ Interactive content concepts
- ◉ Extensive coding knowledge
- ◉ Flexible design orientations

- ◉ Knowledge of colour theory
- ◉ Image optimization
- ◉ Graphic development
- ◉ Web training and instruction

## Related Experience

### Principal Web Designer
AllegRo Consulting, Abbottsford, BC ◉ 2003 to 2008

Founded and operated a successful independent web development and design company, serving client organizations throughout British Columbia. More than 200 websites designed to meet the specific requirements and preferences of private and non-profit sector clients.

- ◉ Demonstrated proficiency and detail orientation with Flash, CSS, PHP and HTML.
- ◉ Provided guidance, support, and training to clients in content development.
- ◉ Managed all aspects of business operations including marketing, bookkeeping, customer service, and quality assurance.
- ◉ Built and maintained strong collaborative working relationships with local web design and web hosting partners.

### Instructor
### Web Technologies Distance Education Program
BC Institute of Technology School of Business, Abbottsford, BC ◉ 2005 to 2008

Provided expertise, instruction, and assessments to students by interfacing with distance education learners via BCIT WebCT.

- ◉ Developed course content and instructed *Introduction to Search Engine Optimization*, member of Assessment Team for grading individual Final Design projects, and Instructor for *Publishing on the Internet 2*.
- ◉ Successfully instructed over 17 class sessions in web design concepts for more than 200 students, and provided additional learning support to students via email and phone.

# Rose Dollinger

*Phone: (250) 456-7651*
*Page 2*

**Design Consultant**
Splash Design, Abbottsford, BC ◉ 1991 to 2001

Consulted with over 250 business, media, and artistic performance clients to produce largely brochure-type websites that incorporated the use of Flash and feedback forums.

◉ Designed and published a unique web-presence for Sea Change Consulting which resulted in a 150% increase in sales within 2 weeks.

◉ In collaboration with Reel to Reel Video Productions, produced a series of 4 "teaser" websites leading up to the launch of Cicero's main web-presence and their Grand Opening.

## Education and Professional Development

**Online Teaching**, BCCAMPUS.CA
Completed 2006

**Associate Certificate in Web Technologies**, British Columbia Institute of Technology
Completed 2002

**Bachelor of Arts, Honours**, University of British Columbia
English and Psychology
Completed 1981

## Professional Affiliations and Memberships

Abbottsford Chamber of Commerce, Abbottsford, BC

Creative Media and Marketing Group, Abbottsford, BC

## Portfolio

http://www.seachange.com/ - Sea Change Consulting

http://www.ciceros.com/ - Cicero's Restaurant

http://www.newhopesociety.com/ - Abbottsford New Hope Society

http://www.compass.com/ - Cultural Compass Clothing

http://www.marionfellon.ca/ - Marion Fellon, performing artist

http://www.moonspa.com/ - Send Me To The Moon Day Spa

# Jennifer Dutchison

P.O. Box 47 • Lansdowne, MD 21227
H: 410-555-3549 • C: 410-555-1000
jen@gmail.com

**Savvy & Bold Business Owner • Talented & Inspired Chef • Events Specialist Competent & Caring Household Manager • Nanny**

## Professional Profile

Dynamic, innovative professional with an eclectic blend of interests and talents serving as the cornerstones for designing, launching, and managing two successful business operations while simultaneously providing private childcare and household management services. Approach every career endeavor with competence, creativity, and seemingly tireless energy.

## Professional Experience

**Greystone Mansion** • www.greystonemansion.com • Baltimore, MD        2004 – Present
Collaborated on the design/build and currently manage an upscale event facility incorporating 7,000 square feet of open space, three acres of professionally landscaped grounds, elegant decor, exquisite bridal room, and a state-of-the-art kitchen.

- Designed optimal kitchen layout to prepare 225 meals within limited space and oversaw six-month construction project, including vendor relations and code inspections.

- Book, plan, and host social and corporate events for up to 225 guests. Market through numerous business alliances, networking, referrals and custom-designed Web site.

- Develop and maintain operating budget; oversee and supervise sub-contractors and groundskeepers, and ensure compliance with all codes and regulations.

- Maintain detailed event records to assist in sales forecasting, strategic business planning, and tracking P & L.

  ★ Established record of excellence and more than doubled annual bookings over three-year period.

  ★ Voted "Best Event Site", 2007 *Baltimore* magazine Baltimore's Hot List.

  ★ Recognized in *Baltimore* magazine, Bridal 2008 issue as, "Best Event Site in the Quad State Area."

**Sugarbaker's Catering** • www.sugarbakers.com • Baltimore, MD        1998 – Present
Founded and independently manage catering company offering festive cuisine and trend-setting food displays for weddings, cocktail parties, business social events and fundraisers. Meet with customers to discuss event specifications, identify theme, and plan menu and décor to reflect customer's style and uniqueness. Design and orchestrate one-of-a kind events at Greystone Mansion or customer's selected venue.

- Recruit temporary personnel to assist with food preparation, service, and clean up. Provide hands-on training and supervision while making best use of individual employee's skills and strengths when delegating assignments.

- Demonstrate extraordinary time management, organizational, and multi-tasking abilities while managing multiple, simultaneous events.

- During recent six-day period, executed events for six different clients, which included planning nine different menus and serving 1275 meals. Catered six-hour breakfast/lunch customer appreciation event for 1100 guests.

  ★ Consistently increase annual sales by as much as 25%.

  ★ Showcased select menus and recipes in *Baltimore* magazine feature articles: "Celebration in the Tropics," Bridal 2007; "A Perfect Finish," Nov 2006; "Brunch without Boundaries," Dec 2005.

  ★ Awarded "Best Display," French Rivera Benefit Dinner, 2007, Towson, MD

**Professional Experience** *(continued)*

**Sommerby's Catering,** Rockville, MD     1998 – 2006
**Deirdre's Catering,** Catonsville, MD     1997 – 2006
**Waverly Inn,** Gaithersburg, MD     1989 – 1999

**Community Experience**

**Valley Health Care Foundation,** Baltimore, MD
- *Chair, Crystal Ball Gala Gift Committee*
  Solicited donated gifts valued between $50 and $5,000 to raise funds for various non-profit organizations. Drafted gift descriptions for event handbook and showcased gifts for maximum visual appeal.

- *Festival of Trees Decorators' Day Event*
  Planned and staged two-hour cooking class to raise funds for the foundation. Creative met the challenge of created menu to serve 30 people with $250 budget.

- *Festival of Trees Display*
  Designed and decorated a tree and table setting, sponsored by Sugarbaker's, which netted $750 proceeds through silent auction.

- *Sugar Plum Ball* (2007)
  Created and developed a theme, menu, and table settings for a father-daughter dinner dance with 176 attendees.

**Youth Ballet of Baltimore, *Board Member,*** Baltimore, MD
- *Chair, Nutcracker Gala* (3 years)
  Developed from concept to full implementation a themed cocktail party fundraiser incorporating silent and live auctions and student ballet performances. Solicited auction items; secured auctioneer and photographer, and arranged press coverage. Served as creative talent and driving force behind event which grew netted proceeds of $6,000 in 2005; $9,000 in 2006; and $15,000 in 2007

**Household Manager / Nanny Experience**

**Doctors Ortega & Cane,** Arlington, VA     1993 – 2007
Provided day-to-day supervision, emotional support, and guidance to three boys, from the time the eldest was two-years old through high school graduation. Began employment as a live-in nanny and reduced hour and days as youth reached maturity.

- Coordinated after-school schedules and activities and provided transportation and supervision for medical appointments, sports, and other extracurricular events.

- Managed basic household activities while parents were working, including grocery shopping and meal preparation for the family.

**Professional Development & Education**

*Devoted hundreds of hours to ongoing professional development throughout career including:*

**Southern Appetizers & Hors d'oeuvres, Sarasota Lodge,** Sarasota, FL    2007
**Remarkable Service, Culinary Cuisine Institute,** Boston, MA    2005
**Modern Day Buffet, Culinary Cuisine Institute,** Boston, MA    2005
**O'Malley's Catering,** Chicago, IL    2004
**Professional Pastry Program, Gourmet Academy,** Dundalk, MD    2000
Credits earned toward associate of arts degree, Loyola College, MD

# MELISSA EDWARDS

424 Waterford Lane ♦ Dallas, TX 75248 ♦ melissa_edwards@hotmail.com ♦ (972) 231-2238

## COMMUNITY RELATIONS

*Community Officer ~ Community Liaison ~ Volunteer Coordinator*

*~ Consistently meet objectives by building and fostering critical community relationships, delivering hands-on executive leadership, and using superior skills in communication, conflict resolution, negotiation, and staff development. ~*

Award-winning, civic-minded leader, public speaker, former educator and entrepreneur. Well-known in the community for distinguished community service/volunteer work and participation on numerous non-profit boards. Public and private-sector experience in effective urban planning initiatives, community outreach, and community development activities.

Goal-oriented, performance-driven professional with 15+ years of progressively responsible experience and a track record of consistently meeting and surpassing objectives regardless of challenges or career transitions. Able to learn quickly and work well with people from diverse socioeconomic groups. Particularly interested in working with government or the arts, or with geriatric population. Proficient in MS Word, Excel & PowerPoint.

**Public Speaking Presentations:**

**KEYNOTE SPEAKER,** American Heart Association Conference, 2001, 200+ attendees
**KEYNOTE SPEAKER,** National AIDS Awareness Conference, 2000, 300+ attendees

## Education

Southern Methodist University (SMU), Dallas, TX
**BACHELOR OF ARTS, PRE-LAW / POLITICAL SCIENCE**

## Demonstrated Success Traits

| | | |
|---|---|---|
| ♦ People-Focused | ♦ Driven & Intuitive | ♦ Excellent Communicator |
| ♦ Principled & Compassionate | ♦ Strategic & Collaborative | ♦ Creative Problem-Solver |
| ♦ Detail-Oriented & Organized | ♦ Analytical & Proactive | ♦ Influential & Inspirational |

## Career Chronology

Bright Star Academy, Dallas, Texas                                                                                     2002–Present
*~ Charter school serving about 500 disadvantaged children in grades K–6. ~*
**CONTRACT CONSULTANT**
**READING FIRST COACH**
**READING INTERVENTIONIST**
Recruited from corporate world to become a Reading Interventionist. Challenged to write a federal grant for the No Child Left Behind (NCLB) program with no previous grant-writing experience. Assisted with writing internal/external communications, press releases, school newsletters, speeches, issuing statements, and letters of recommendation. Worked with special education teacher and parents to coordinate support services for children with dyslexia and special needs and ensured they received necessary services.

♦ Succeeded in securing five-year $1 million grant from State of Texas' Reading First (NCLB) Program and was immediately promoted to Reading First Coach.
♦ Increased 3rd-attempt TAKS pass/fail rate for 3rd grade non-performing and at-risk students to 100% for academic years 2004 and 2005, and 95% for 2006.

<u>Bright Star Academy</u> (Continued)
- ♦ Played a key role in school receiving Gold Medal Performance Award from Texas Education Agency for achievement in reading and math, 2004, for 1st time in school's existence.
- ♦ Worked closely with Urban Planner to ensure code compliance and prepare package to renew Special Use Permit (SUP). Succeeded in securing City Council's approval of SUP every 2 years.
- ♦ Praised for coordinating well-received special-event projects, committee assignments, and community outreach activities. Secured holiday food drive donations from leading grocery stores and secured sponsors to adopt 25 families and purchase toys for underprivileged children.
- ♦ Trained team of 12 teachers, 5 paraprofessionals and charter school administrative staff to analyze student achievement and provide interventional support for students reading 1 grade or more below grade level.

<u>The Glisten Group</u>, Dallas, Texas                                                       1986–2002
*~ Commercial cleaning company serving several high-profile Fortune 500 accounts. ~*

**CHIEF EXECUTIVE OFFICE**
Built company from the ground up. Started with 2 employees and grew staff to 65. Managed P&L, hiring, training, problem resolution, and sales. Negotiated all contracts. Worked with and trained all employees. Provided world-class customer service. Provided staff with full benefits from Day 1.

- ♦ Grew annual sales from zero to $800,000. Sold company for a substantial profit.
- ♦ Maintained 100% perfect OSHA safety record. Never had a single accident.
- ♦ Consistently generated about 50% of new business from customer referrals.
- ♦ Secured lucrative contracts with customers including: American Airlines, DART, Century 21, Trammell Crow, Austin Industries, Continental Trailways, Southwestern Bell, Host International, McInnis Real Estate, and Henry S. Miller.

**Honors and Awards**_____

**Recognition of Valuable Contributions,** <u>Bright Star Academy</u>, 2006
**Outstanding Achievement Award,** <u>Bright Star Academy</u>, 2005
**Outstanding Achievement Award,** <u>Bright Star Academy</u>, 2003

**21st Century Most Promising Leader Award,** 2004

**Ring of Honor Inductee for Outstanding Leadership,** <u>Dallas Urban League Guild</u>, 2006

**Board Memberships, Professional Affiliations, and Volunteer Activities**_____

- ♦ **Former Advisory Board Member,** <u>American Heart Association</u>
- ♦ **Former Board Member,** <u>City of Dallas MLK, Jr. Family Health Clinic</u>
- ♦ **Former Board Member,** <u>City of Dallas Urban Rehabilitation Standards Board</u>
- ♦ **Former Board Member,** <u>City of Dallas Health & Human Services Commission</u>
- ♦ **Former Board Member,** <u>City of Dallas Tax & Equalization Board</u>
- ♦ **Former Board Member,** <u>City of Dallas South Dallas/Fair Park Trust Fund Board</u>
- ♦ **Former Board Member,** <u>Southern Women's League Fighting AIDS in US</u>

- ♦ **Member,** <u>Alpha Kappa Alpha Sorority</u>       ♦ **Volunteer,** <u>The Science Place</u>
- ♦ **Member,** <u>Lambda Legal, Liberty Circle</u>       ♦ **Volunteer,** <u>The United Way</u>

## INNOVATIVE QUALITY CONTROL MANAGER

### *LEADERSHIP PROFILE*

Dedicated Quality Assurance Professional with over 10 years of successful career progression in quality optimization and operations management. Proven performer who transitions easily from vision and strategy to implementation and follow through. Focused on adhering to organizational missions and philosophy while positively impacting bottom line and daily performance. Recipient of multiple company awards for superior leadership, technical expertise and innovative contributions.

❖ **Quality Control** ❖ **Product Development** ❖ **Vendor Relations** ❖
❖ **Technical Analysis** ❖ **Internal Auditing** ❖ **Project Management** ❖
❖ **Performance Testing** ❖ **Budget Planning** ❖ **Process Improvement** ❖
❖ **Problem Resolution** ❖ **Cost Control** ❖ **Team Building** ❖

### *KEY PERFORMANCE INDICATORS*

- Spearheaded ISO9001 certification project; certification granted on first attempt.
- Stabilized vendor relations smoothing product flow; increased revenue by 7%.
- Implemented process refinement, improving discard rate from 18% to 2%.
- Instituted team concept work philosophy, doubling staff performance efficiency.
- Elevated total product quality by 10% through strict adherence to methodologies.
- Increased customer satisfaction by 20% by implementing timely delivery process.
- Authored standard operating procedures manual for 100% training consistency.
- Conducted plant visits and tours for customers, elevating company credibility.
- Initiated installation of computerized audit stations reducing test time by 24%.
- Interfaced with senior managers successfully attaining highest profits in five years.

## CAREER DIGEST

**ABC METALS,** Concord ON                                         **1998 – Present**
*North American manufacturer of thermoplastic injection moulded components and assemblies specifically for the automotive industry offering 30 leading product lines. Annual revenues in excess of $180 Million. A division of the worldwide Fortune 200 Company, ABC Tool Works.*

**Quality Control Supervisor**                                    2005 – Present
Promoted to direct and lead a 23 person team of Technicians and Assemblers responsible for quality assurance and acceptance testing for the various lines of products. Act as a hands-on leader and mentor to staff while maintaining positive relationships with vendors and customers.
*Career Advancement:*
 • Identified as the leading successor for the Quality Control Manager role.

**Quality Technician**                                            2000 – 2005
Appointed to perform a variety of inspection related duties and testing on incoming materials and outgoing products to ensure compliance with quality assurance system requirements. Analyze and compile data for the preparation of statistical reports.
*Career Advancement:*
 • Promoted to Quality Control Supervisor through outstanding performance.

**Machine Operator**                                             1998 – 2000
Hired to operate and maintain conventional, special purpose and injection-moulding machinery. Responsible for setting up all machines to produce quality products.
*Career Advancement:*
 • Appointed as Quality Technician. Recognized for dedication and taking iniative.

## EDUCATION

**Certificate - *Certified ISO 9001 Auditor,*** York University                 2006
 • Achieved honourable standing while working on a full time basis.
**Certificate - *Business and Commerce,*** Dunlap School of Business            2000
 • Awarded Dunlap Leaders Bursary for outstanding academic achievement.

## COMPUTER SKILLS

Expert computer proficiency in MS Office programs and quality control systems.

# Stephen Fu

P.O. Box 122  ·  Wilmington, NC 28401
H: 910-555-4998  ·  stevfu@gmail.com  ·  C: 910-555-9500

*Seeking federal, state, or county career opportunity targeting environmental epidemiology, natural science, or conservation*

## IMMEDIATE VALUE OFFERED

Meticulous attention to detail and accuracy, intuitive and analytical thinking, and demonstrated ability for observing and collecting data are cornerstones of honorary academic achievements and practical hands-on experience in the environmental, chemical, and biological sciences field.

- A versatile, adaptable professional and seemingly inexhaustible investigator of facts who pursues all possible avenues to solve problems. Strong technical writing skills and ability to communicate technical information to non-technical users.

- Experience researching, analyzing and summarizing various technical and scientific literature and reports—USGS database, Endangered Species Act, National Park Service, Department of Interior, Medical Journals—to prepare and present information for academic credit.

- Laboratory and computer proficiency. Skilled in use of wet laboratory techniques for physical and chemical analysis; basic knowledge of HPLC, GC and other instrumentation. Experience with multiple-step chemical and biological testing procedures. Proficient in MS Office applications; working knowledge of SPSS statistical software.

- Proven team commitment. Skilled in supporting managers, colleagues, and consumers by asking good questions to gain critical information and deliver tangible results. Set high standards for self and others to produce accurate, compliant documentation and follow set procedures.

## EDUCATION

**B.S., Biology, *University of North Carolina at Wilmington***, Wilmington, NC – May 2007

**Significant Coursework**: Botany · Ecology · Histology · Biochemistry · Statistical Research Methods · General and Organic Chemistry · Immunology · Conservation Biology · Toxicology · Environmental Science

### Select Academic Achievements

- Conducted critical analysis of air and water quality at Cape Lookout National Seashore to assess areas of major concern. Utilized various print and Internet resources including Federal Endangered Species Act, National Park Services Plan-of-Action, and a Natural Resource Assessment for Cape Lookout National Seashore Technical Report.

- Researched Centers for Disease Control and Prevention (CDC) literature to prepare toxicological profile on chemical warfare agent tabun and delivered informative presentation to professor and classmates.

- Reviewed and synthesized technical literature to create complex annotated bibliography for biology professor for pending publication regarding "heavy metals as suspected endocrine distributors."

- Took initiative to draft standard operating procedures (SOPs) for the University chemistry and biology labs that provided guidelines for students, increased lab safety and efficiency, and decreased costs.

- Simulated a hydrologic forecast for environmental science class utilizing United States Geological Survey (USGS) database and US census data.

- Prepared environmental impact statement and species recovery plan arguing potential demise of pyramid snail.

- Actively involved in collecting data to support a graduate student's research project, in cooperation with National Park Service, regarding fresh water quality on the Pamlico Sound.

*Member of Chi Beta Phi honorary science and math fraternity – Alpha Epsilon Charter, University of North Carolina*

### PROFESSIONAL EXPERIENCE

**Various Academic Internships**                                       1998–2003

Completed numerous one- to six-month assignments and gained real-world experience while pursuing credits from University of North Carolina at Wilmington (Wilmington, NC) for degree in pharmacy. Acquired broad scope of business management, laboratory, customer service, patient education, and medical team support experience through practical assignments at numerous hospital, community and retail pharmacies, research facilities, and government-funded medical centers.

**Key Business Sites:** *Veterans Administration Hospital*, Wilmington, NC; *Cooper's Pharmacy,* Cape Lookout, NC; *Myrtle Beach Hospital Center*, Myrtle Beach, SC; *Raleigh Medical Center*, Raleigh, NC; *Eastern Medical*; Goldsboro, NC; *Tri-Quad Labs*; Greenville, NC.

- Monitored and managed laboratory data for 20-35 VA hospital patients to determine correct dosage levels of anticoagulation drug.

- Prepared intravenous medications under sterile laboratory conditions for a hospital pharmacy.

- Counseled mixed diversity of patients on appropriate use of prescription and over-the-counter medications.

- Collected and analyzed data pertaining to NSAID drug utilization and presented findings to pharmacy and medical staff. Resulting changes in therapy guidelines decreased number of duplicate prescriptions, reduced incidence of medical complications, and produced significant business cost savings.

- Researched alternative drug therapy for terminally ill cancer patients to assess most effective treatment for controlling pain while reducing costs. Supported medical oncologist by answering questions related to medications.

- Assisted pharmacist with preparation of radioisotopes for nuclear medicine. Performed calculations of cyclotron operation time. Monitored radiation levels in accordance with Nuclear Regulatory Commission guidelines.

- Demonstrated basic business management skills by supporting day-to-day operations and customer service at various pharmacies.

### MILITARY EXPERIENCE

**United States Army**                                                   1990–1996

Honorably discharged, E-4. Completed basic training at Ft. Bragg, NC; assigned to Explosive Ordnance Disposal, and deployed stateside and in Germany.

# Carol Grande

1888 Goosedown Road   Mentor, Ohio  44060     PH: 440-357-1234

NEW GRADUATE

## Medical Billing Coding Specialist

---

**At Home Professionals**
Ft. Collins, Colorado

Diploma - June 2005

Final Score - 96%

---

### SELECTED COURSEWORK

- Medical Terminology

- Diagnostic Coding

- Procedural Coding

- Anatomy and Physiology

- Medical Claims Procedures

- Medical Ethics

- Legal Issues of Profession

*"Congratulations on completing your course! ...Your hard work and determination...will help you be successful in your new career."*

- Executive Director,
At Home Professionals

*" Carol has exceptional medical – billing skills...she has demonstrated her qualification for handling your medical claims & billing needs... an asset in any medical office"*

- Graduate Counselor,
At Home Professionals

*...brings fourteen years of medical experience combined with a high level of commitment and dedication to the position of*

## MEDICAL BILLING SPECIALIST

### Professional Strengths

*Ability to seek and thoroughly analyze information to make tough decisions... ...Uses balanced judgment while displaying empathy and sensitivity to others experiencing difficulties...Brings stability to the entire team...Displays persistent and perseverance in approach to achieving goals.*

### ACHIEVEMENTS

➢ Evaluated abnormal behavior of parent and determined the presence of heart attack symptoms. The accurate conclusion and immediate reaction to her condition resulted in timely, life – saving treatment.

➢ Recommended appropriate treatment to hospital patients as a result of accurate monitoring of vital signs: blood pressure, temperature and urinalysis.

➢ Effectively trained new nursing assistants while on the job in addition to regular responsibilities to assist new staff in accurately learning new position.

➢ Utilized proper sterilization techniques to clean wounds reducing patient's risk of infection.

➢ Conducted inspections of patient's bed and living area to confirm acceptable sanitation standards eliminating local and cross contamination.

### RELATED VOLUNTEER EXPERIENCE

#### A COMMIT TO BE FIT

Volunteer – generated donations from sponsors for cardiac care.

Breast Foundation – enhanced awareness and generated donations toward research for the Breast Cancer Foundation.

### EMPLOYMENT EXPERIENCE

**Nursing Assistant**                                 *October 1990 – December 1999*

Hershey Medical Center - Hershey, Pennsylvania

- ✓ Entered labs in computer
- ✓ Ordered supplies for patients
- ✓ Operated a Hoyer lift machine

**Nursing Assistant**                                          *June 1986 – October 1990*

Patterson Nursing Home - Wheeling, West Virginia

- ✓ Operated a Hoyer Lift machine.
- ✓ Monitored and cared for patients.
- ✓ Maintained reports and records of facility conditions.

# Michelle Hiscock

5555 Tanner Road, Prince Rupert, BC, V5Y 9E9
Home: (250) 627-4421• Cell: (250) 431-2300
Email: michelleh@shaw.com

## Youth-At-Risk Support Specialist

*"Promoting and supporting positive changes in clients' lives."*

A compassionate mentor and role model with 8 years of experience supporting high-risk and at-risk youth, and their families. A self-motivated leader with a capacity for creative program development and adaptation. Commitment to collaborative problem solving within multi-disciplinary teams to turn strategies into results. Verifiable talent for performing well in emotionally-charged settings to engage hard to reach youth of all circumstances.

## Work Experience

**Youth Care Worker, Independent Living Program**              2005 to Present
Prince Rupert Contact Line and Centre Society (PRCLCS)

Working with at-risk youth referred by the Ministry of Children and Families (MCFD) aged 16-19, performing life skill assessments, creating learning plans, developing life skills, and supporting youth towards independence.

➤ Working with 12 clients per month on average and periodically with approximately 40 clients per month who will join the program at age 16.

➤ Successfully developed and initiated the Community Kitchen Program in 2007 to encourage life skill development and establish a foundation for peer support among program clients.

➤ Proven expertise in crises intervention, program implementation, liaising with Ministry representatives, and supervising weekend relief staff.

**Family Support Worker, Homefront Program**              2001 to 2005
Prince Rupert Contact Line and Centre Society (PRCLCS)

Worked with children in care of MCFD or at risk of being in care, and their parents. Provided additional support to individual children living with mental illness, addictions or special needs. Transported and supervised children for family visitations.

➤ Worked with clients and their families for 4 years facilitating 1 family reunification in 40, as warranted.

➤ Built parenting capacity with clients' families by applying assessment tools and providing parenting skills instruction.

➤ Functioned autonomously to expedite solutions while liaising with officers of MCFD and PRCLCS to provide regular progress reports.

**Mental Health Care Worker/Community Living Support Worker**              1999 to 2005
Prince Rupert Contact Line and Centre Society (PRCLCS)

Worked 1:1 with adults living with chronic mental illness to meet life skill goals outlined in MCFD support contracts and to move clients towards independent or semi-independent community living.

➤ Worked with a 25 clients per month on average, facilitated opportunities for clients to practice budgeting, medication management, and other life skills essential for independent living.

➤ Established the Peer Interaction Program at the Prince Rupert Contact Line Activity Centre in 2002 which increased social opportunities for clients.

**Intensive Support and Supervision Worker**
Prince Rupert Youth Resources

As and when required
2001 to Present

Working 1:1 on a contract basis with high-risk youth referred for Intensive Support and Supervision by MCFD as an alternative to custody, or as a condition of Probation Orders and providing progress reports to the referring Youth Probation Officers.

- ➢ Monitoring clients' strict adherence to Probation Orders.
- ➢ Supporting clients towards healthy and safe living through role modeling, peer links, and school credit work programs.
- ➢ Bonding with clients and applying creative problem solving skills to focus them on new behaviours.
- ➢ Facilitating and supervising time at home with family for clients.
- ➢ Successful removal of up to 50% of clients from the Justice System over 5 years of post-program living.

## Administrative Skills

A multi-skilled organizer with experience administering financial processes, supervising staff and mentoring students. Fully proficient with computers and a variety of office equipment. Ability to gather, analyse and roll up data to produce a variety of meaningful reports. Exceptional verbal and written communication skills.

## Education

**Bachelor of Arts, Psychology Major**, Graduated 1999
University of British Columbia

**Justice Institute of British Columbia Training**

Adult Probation Officer Training:
- The Adult Probation Officer and Community Corrections (AP 151), 2007
- Adult Probation and Criminal Court Process (AP 152), 2007
- Sentencing Options and Post Sentence Supervision Orders (APO 153), 2007
- Professional Ethics and Standards of Conduct (Community) (APO 154), 2007

Youth Probation Officer Training:
- Overview of the Youth Criminal Justice System (YPO 101), 2007
- Overview of the Youth Criminal Justice Act (YPO 102), 2007

Dealing with Interpersonal Conflict, 2007
Effects of Separation and Divorce on Children, 2007
Advanced Intensive Support and Supervision Training, 2003
Intensive Support and Supervision Training, 2002

**Professional Development**

Alcohol and Drug Course for Youth Practitioners – John Hattan & Associates
Non-Violent Crisis Intervention – Northern Health Authority
Fetal Alcohol Spectrum Disorder Training Sessions – The Friendship Centre
Teaching Pro-Social Behaviour to Anti-Social Youth – John Hattan & Associates
Promoting Healthy Bodies – Prince Rupert Recreation Centre
Occupational First Aid Level 1 – St. John's Ambulance
Food Safe Level 1 – Food Safe Secretariat

Michelle Hiscock
Ph: (250) 627-4421

# Nanette Holt, M.A.

1234 San Anselmo Avenue, San Francisco, CA 94102 • 415-123-4567 • info@theresumestudio.com

*Fundraising • Community Leadership • Boards, Councils & Bureaus*

Seasoned volunteer with 18 years of diverse nonprofit fundraising / leadership experience coupled with donor cultivation and event planning experience, and commitment to philanthropic activities. Interest in legal, ethical, historical, and cultural perspectives related to philanthropy. Pre-nonprofit experience includes newspaper reporter / editor positions.

**Objective:** To earn an *Executive Master of Arts Degree in Philanthropic Studies* at Columbia University.

Resourceful, focused, and persuasive communicator. Innovative problem-solver with growing appreciation for the development of mutually beneficial community-based partnerships. Proven ability to lead and think clearly under pressure.

## NONPROFIT EXPERIENCE

### Fundraising

- **2006 Tennis Invitational Event Committee,** United Way, Greater Bay Area, present. Serving on one of two principle annual fundraising events, which generated $800,000 last year. Duties include development of corporate sponsorships ranging from $3,500 to $50,000 and acquisition of auction items valued up to $25,000. Additonal objectives include table sales and bidder cultivation.

- **Smith Kelin Foundation, Founder,** San Francisco State University, San Francisco, 1998. Fund honored memory of treasured academic and awarded scholarships to promising young writers, providing the opportunity to study in SF State's summer writing program.

- **Fundraising Co-chair,** South Bay Junior Academy, PTA, Torrance, California, 1992–1994. Co-managed, directed, and publicized events. Led the development, coordination, and leadership of volunteers, raising $60,000 annually through golf tournaments, auctions, carnivals, and book fairs.

### Committees, Councils & Boards

- **Executive Board Member / Chair,** Academic Boosters, PTA, Francisco Middle School, San Francisco, 1994–1996, 1998–2000. Led four annual fund campaigns designed to reduce class sizes. Exceeded fundraising goals, raising $86,500 annually. Recruited and managed 24 volunteers. Authored and oversaw logistics related to community annual appeal letter.

- **Board Member,** Smith Kelin Foundation, SF State University, 1998. Created scholarship recipient evaluation and reward process and helped revenues surpass forecast figures. Fund active through 2003.

- **Member,** School Site Council, South Bay Junior Academy, Torrance, California, 1993–1994. One of only two parents school-wide to help manage $76,330 budget annually, working with council members to allocate spending for funding awarded by the state.

- **Speakers Bureau Member,** United Way, Greater Bay Area, 2005–present. One of 12 speakers representing United Way to current and potential corporate donors.

### Community

- **Producer,** Torrance, California, 1995. Public and private painting / sculpture exhibitions raising cancer care funds for Torrance, California teacher. Recruited and managed 10 volunteers, oversaw publicity and budget from conception to cleanup.

- **Campaign Designer / Producer,** South Bay Junior Academy, Torrance, California, 1994. School-wide bicycle helmet safety initiative.

- **Wish Grantor,** United Way, Greater Bay Area, 1998–present.

———————————— PROFESSIONAL EXPERIENCE ————————————

**Vice President** and **Board of Directors Member,** ABC Warehousing Co., Torrance, California 1988–2001

**Assistant to Volunteer Director,** Mercedes and Linux ATP Men's Tennis Tournaments, San Francisco / Santa Clara, California, 1992–1995.
- Assisted in the management of 350 volunteers.

**Editor,** Feature Section, Wapakoneta Tribune, Wapakoneta, Ohio, 1982–1984
- Feature section awarded for excellence in 1983 by Ohio Newspaper Publishers' Association

**Reporter,** Wapakoneta Tribune, Wapakoneta, Ohio, 1980–1982

**Reporter,** Big City News Service, Dayton, Ohio, 1979–1980

———————————— EDUCATION & PROFESSIONAL DEVELOPMENT ————————————

**Master of Arts, School of Journalism and Communication, 1979**
Ohio University, Athens, Ohio
- Research Assistant
- Faculty Search Committee Member
  *One of two graduate students representing the School of Journalism and working closely with dean of Journalism school to evaluate and hire professors.*

**Bachelor of Arts, Literature, 1975**
University of Minnesota, Twin Cities, Minnesota
- One year study abroad program, England / Denmark

**The Foundation Center, San Francisco, California, 2005**
- Grant Seeking Basics
- Making the Ask
- Proposal Writing Basics
- Proposal Budgeting Basics

**Compass Point, San Francisco, California, 2005**
- Fundraising with Special Events

1234 San Anselmo Avenue, San Francisco, CA 94102 • 415-123-4567 • info@theresumestudio.com

# JOHN JOBSEEKER

City, State - USA ■ Phone: 888-295-4985 ■ E-mail: info@resumeasap.com

## Results-Oriented Telecommute Professional
*Offering Nearly 20 Years of Management & Sales Experience*

**Profile**

Resourceful business professional with a diversified and solid career characterized by a broad range of experience in hospitality, retail, and sales/lending management. Respected leader known for creative problem solving and the ability to generate consensus within a group. Career chronicled by multiple promotions, recognized achievements, and superior-rated performance. Strong recruitment, training, and team-motivational skills.

Expert communicator with the demonstrated ability to discern customer needs, devise customized solutions to meet specific objectives, and develop strong partnering relationships with key decision makers. Adept in directing multiple, competing priorities.

**Expertise**

**Management:** Staff supervision, budget management, purchasing, cost control strategies, contract negotiations, operations management, process improvement, organization, time management, vendor relations.

**Sales:** Marketing initiatives, needs analysis, lead generation, new business development, presentations, problem solving, customer satisfaction.

**Training:** Training manuals, employee handbooks, new hire orientations, compensation/incentive programs, policy implementation.

**Career Progression**

MAJOR UNIVERSITY – City, ST
**Academic Advisor / Recruiter**, 5/2008 to Present
Recruit, advise, and enroll students in graduate and undergraduate academic programs. Counsel potential students regarding admissions and degree requirements. Verify enrollment status and ensure students are being placed in appropriate courses.

MAJOR LENDING INSTITUTION – City, ST
**Account Executive**, 7/2007 to 2/2008
Implemented sales strategies to work with clients in originating business. Conducted client meetings to instruct on processes and guidelines to ensure that business conformed to client needs and company guidelines. Communicated loan status to brokers from pre-qualification, submission, underwriting, to closing. Reviewed files to ensure proper completion and follow through to closing.
Key Accomplishments:
■ Monthly sales +$1M consistently starting the first month after training.

REGIONAL LENDING INSTITUTION – City, ST
**Vice President of Operations**, 4/2003 to 5/2007
Hired, trained, and mentored operational staff. Analyzed workflow and monitored employee production daily; responsible for maintaining effective levels of communication, service level agreements, and cooperation of staff in multiple departments. Actively maintained highest possible service levels both internally and externally. Acted as interdepartmental liaison to facilitate effective communication between all levels of management.

**Appendix B: Resume and Cover Letter Samples**

*Regional Lending Institution Continued...*

Key Accomplishments:

- Developed a process to ensure compliance standards were met according to company, state, and federal guidelines.
- Considered an integral part of the development team for PMC Lending; worked as a loan officer and underwriter before being promoted to Vice President of Operations.
- Implemented training programs and job descriptions for each position.

REGIONAL SALON – City, ST
**President / Owner**, 10/2001 to 10/2003
Directed daily operations of a full service salon.

Key Accomplishments:

- Purchased the salon immediately following September 11, 2001 when business was declining. Rapidly increased sales 65% by setting performance levels to achieve sales volume and profit objectives.
- Recruited and hired a talented staff of hair designers and increased the clientele by 40% in one year.
- With an innovative approach to increasing operating efficiency, was able to sell the business making those two years very profitable.

REGIONAL STAFFING AGENCY – City, ST
**Assistant Branch Manager**, 3/1999 to 10/2001
Coordinated staffing office, which offered placement for local companies and national firms such as Walt Disney World, Sea World, Universal Studios, and other hospitality venues. Supervised payroll, hiring, and training for employees. Managed sales team and oversaw human resources duties. Maintained high levels of communication between corporate office and local branch.

Key Accomplishments:

- Suggested an automatic dialer system to be implemented company wide to save time and allow more productivity on other tasks.

MAJOR HOTEL CHAIN – City, ST
**Food and Beverage Manager**, 12/1989 to 7/1999
Managed several departments including room service, lobby, bar, restaurants, and banquets. Hired, trained, evaluated, and terminated employees. Maintained a high level of communication between departments and managers.

Key Accomplishments:

- Organized and managed the best city wide brunch for three years in a row.
- Promoted several contests with the staff to encourage sales and repeat business.

## Education

University Name – City, ST
**Bachelor's Degree** – Business Management, expected completion: 2009

University Name – City, ST
**Associate's Degree** – Business Management, 1999

# DAVID P. JOHNSON

806.834.8003 ■ david.johnson@gmail.com
5530 Circle Court ■ Ashton, IL 33019

## SENIOR SALES PROFESSIONAL                    LIGHTING CERTIFIED (LC)

**National Sales – Product Management – Business Development – Project Management**

More than 15-year record in the lighting industry with background in all phases, including lamp construction, managing high-profile, Fortune 100 OEM and B2B accounts. Led sales teams of 50-60 people – up to 15 direct reports. Strengths in long-term relationship building, consultative sales strategies, and product migration.

**THE 80% CONVERTER:**          Combining precision-targeting, in-depth needs analysis, and expert product knowledge to consistently convert 80% of prospects, increase margins, and exceed quota.

Thrived in industry's most challenging sales environment (Holophane) with highly complex go-to-market method selling to all cross-disciplinary project members:

- ➤ **Navigating complex, multi-year project cycles from concept to finalization.**
- ➤ **Negotiating with and selling to government organizations ( including DOT) and municipalities.**
- ➤ **Driving margin growth while building legacy accounts for premium brand – up to $1M in revenues.**

Proficient in Dodge Reports (marketing and sales research), and CRM software, i.e. Goldmine, Lotus Notes, and Pivotal. Advanced skills in Chief Architect and AutoCAD-based photometric construction and design.

- Hold bachelor's degree in Economics -

## EXPERIENCE & ACHIEVEMENTS

**A.B. LIGHTING,** Davenport, IL (telecommuted from home office)                    2002 to 9/2007
*(International leader in lighting solutions for industrial, emergency, and outdoor applications.)*
**Factory Sales Engineer – Lighting**

Hired to manage high-growth southwest Wisconsin and northern Illinois territory. Targeted specifiers, architects, landscape architects, consulting engineers, and interior lighting designers .

- **Maintained 80% conversion rate** – exceeding most peers, drawing upon solid experience, accurately identifying, targeting, and selling to realistic markets/customers.
- **Tripled number of specifiers approached,** previously unaware of Holophane brand.
- **Grew account from zero to $400K in 3 years, capturing 20% yearly sales increase while establishing legacy accounts:**
  - Realized margin of 5-8% higher than peers on premium brands having minimum set margins.
  - Sold to and coordinated all stakeholders within process/project: from engineer, contractor, distribution, and end-user.
  - **Secured initial sales and established legacy accounts** with Certco, Owens Corning and Rock Valley College Library(indoor lighting); and Sun Prairie, Beloit, and Evansville, (street lighting), **delivering combined $1M- in revenues.**

|  | 2003 | 2004 | 2005 |
|---|---|---|---|
| Revenue | $300K | $400K | $500K |
| *Increase* | *+5%* | *+8%* | *+5%* |

**GETTERS INTERNATIONAL, INC.,** Provo, UT                    2000 to 2002

*(Global leader and pioneer in commercialization of getter, gas purification, and trace impurity analysis technology for industrial applications.)*

**Applications Engineer**

**Drove revenues, reengineered service processes, and added new third-tier, niche-market customers.**
Representative clients included Fortune 100s such as Osram Sylvania, Philips, GE, and Venture (OEM lamp manufacturers). Teamed with physicists and engineers to match product solutions to clients' high-speed manufacturing needs in ISO 9000/14000 environment. Developed sales and rollout plan for patented products throughout North America.

- **Delivered growth from $1.8M to $2.16M** (20% sales increase) during economic downturn.
- Transformed service processes to highlight technical product advantages, performance increases, and cost savings, resulting in successful acquisition and outsourcing of Osram Sylvania's getter/giver processes business.
- **Migrated first-tier clients from older to newer technology 6 months ahead of schedule:**
    - Converted 2 of the "Big Three" lighting companies to new product and delivered $1M+ in annual sales from Philips ($200K+ increase from $800K).

**INDEPENDENT MANUFACTURERS' REPRESENTATIVE**                          1990 to 1999
*(Managed sales efforts for companies in refractory metals, industrial ceramics, and lighting industries.)*

**Sales Engineer / Product Consultant / Product Manager**

Managed existing B2B and OEM accounts and acquired new business using multi-channel prospecting, telemarketing, and cold calling strategies. Performed market research as basis for new product development recommendations to management. Served as corporate representative at seminars, conferences, and trade shows. Supervised up to 10 sales representatives.

- **Seized $2M in revenues** in 8-state Midwest territory by building sales of emerging, high-tech products for GTE Sylvania.
- **Rocketed territories from the ground up to $1M+ in annual sales** in 7-state Midwest region within 8 years with several product lines.
- **Shortened order lifecycle time from 2 weeks to 4 days** by implementing regional inventory plan.

---

## EDUCATION, CERTIFICATION & AFFILIATION

**Lighting Certified (LC), 2006**
National Council on Qualifications for the Lighting Professions (NCQLP)

**Bachelor of Science degree in Economics,** concentration in HR, Labor, and General Business
UNIVERSITY OF ILLINOIS, Chicago, IL

- Secretary/Treasurer: Illuminating Engineering Society of North America (IESNA), Ashton Section, since 2006
- Industry contributor to Wisconsin Focus on Energy lighting incentives program guidelines.
- Member: Greater Ashton Chamber of Commerce.

# CHRISTOPHER JOHNSTON

christopherjohnston@hotmail.com

8472 Liverpool Lane
Apollo Beach, Florida 33742

**·····**

Home: (813) 645-0094
Cellular: (813) 645-0095

## AREA MANAGER/ PROJECT MANAGER

### Offering 10+ Years' Residential Construction Experience

~ Known for unwavering integrity, outstanding attention to detail, uncompromising dependability, and stellar ability to build strong relationships, resolve problems, and thrive in fast-paced environments. ~

- **Respected Industry Leader and Manager:** Consistently recognized as the "go-to guy" who completes projects on time or early, with exceptional quality, and provides outstanding customer service. Characterized as a fair, open-minded, results-driven manager who coaches, supervises, and motivates staff members to achieve and exceed expectations. ... *Praised by senior management for leadership skills. ... Two-Time Employee of the Month, 2005 and 2006. ... Received Numerous "Certificates of Appreciation."*

- **Superior Ability to Meet Client Needs:** Regularly receive letters of appreciation from customers, supervisors, and senior management commending professionalism, responsiveness, competence, and customer service excellence. ... *"I will always remember how Christopher Johnston went that extra step ... because of him that our first building experience was truly rewarding," F. Boyd, Home Buyer.*

- **State Licensed General Contractor, Florida:** Extensive knowledge of residential construction and demonstrated ability to achieve exemplary quality standards.

- **Qualified Stormwater Management Inspector:** Certified by Florida Department of Environmental Protection.

## CORE COMPETENCIES

Area Management ... Project Management ... Quality Control ... Process Control ... Trade Partner Relations ... Evenflow Construction Implementation ... Bottleneck Identification / Exploitation ... Risk Management ... Material Shortage Procurement ... Meeting and Weekly Start Meeting Facilitation ... Safety Compliance ... Value Generating Process Improvements ... Minimize Cost / Pricing Variances ... Cycle Time Reduction and Control ... Pre-Construction Site Conditions ... Negotiation ... Rapport Building ... Quality Customer Service ... Sales Center Updates ... Product Modifications ... Construction Superintendent Supervision ... Internal Company Communications ... Closed-Loop Trade Partner Meetings ... Quality Control Program Implementation ... Central Scheduling Management ... Closing Department Management ... Staff Training and Development ... Scheduling and Supervision ... Report Generation ... New Initiative Rollout and Implementation ... Auto-Pay Management

**Computer Software:** MS Word, Primavera, Hyphen Solutions Build Pro

## EXPERIENCE

PULTE, Tampa, Florida                                                                                    2006 – 2007
**Area Manager Two**
Manage two large-scale master-planned sub-divisions in Florida. Employment ended on good terms after merger between Lennar and US Homes resulted in a workforce reduction; both Director of Operations and Division President praised integrity and leadership at time of release and indicated eligibility for rehire.

- Managed, supervised, and developed four to nine Construction Superintendents.
- Successfully met Director of Operations' challenge to close homes scheduled for June in May; reduced cycle time to meet the challenge, allowing region to make numbers; met 100% of pushed-ahead close dates.
- Recognized as a key contributor in raising Tampa's JD Powers scores during a depressed housing market.
- Lowered construction cost variances below standard industry expectations.
- Consistently met budget guidelines and 100% of closing dates, completing projects on time or early.

# CHRISTOPHER JOHNSTON

■■■■■

... Continued ...

CENTEX HOMES, Weston and Tampa, Florida  1998 – 2006
**Assistant Project Manager / Closing Manager, Rivercreek** (2005 – 2006)
**Process Control Manager** (2002 – 2006)

As multi-tasking skills became evident, senior management gradually added Closing Manager and Assistant Project Manager responsibilities. Competently managed three concurrent positions for 1,382-unit residential community. Managed, supervised, and developed up to 15 Construction Superintendents. Supervised 5-6 people in the closing department, including closing administrators and assistants; department generated a record 492 closings in 2005.

Endorsed and vetoed trade partners. Ensured materials were procured even during shortages by working closely with suppliers. Dealt with brokers, loan applications, and credit issues. Actively identified and exploited bottlenecks. Documented as the "primary qualifier" on all permits from 2003–2005. Reported to Divisional Project Manager.

- Met challenge of securing an alternate concrete source during the concrete shortage of 2004/2005—in only one day—when then-current provider communicated their inability to supply concrete for 14 new homes a week; division was the only one company-wide that experienced absolutely no curtailing of construction.
- Recognized within company as a key contributor in Centex's ability to pull more permits and close more homes in Tampa than any other single builder for two years running, as documented by Metro Study.
- Communicated needs to trade partners and implemented Evenflow Construction principles, garnering trust and respect of trade partners.
- Twice awarded "Employee of the Month," in 2005 and 2006.
- Routinely received top performance rating of "5" for consistent ability to meet and exceed expectations.

**Full Superintendent** (2000 – 2002)
- Recognized as the first-ever in Weston division to achieve 100% score rating on a multi-family town home.
- Consistently received high marks on reviews and praise from customers and senior management for workmanship, customer service, and ability to bring quality projects in on time or ahead of schedule.

**Assistant Superintendent** (2000 – 2000)
- Scored flawless 100% rating on very first home, an extremely rare occurrence.
- Achieved fast-track 90-day promotion to Full Superintendent based on quality of work, ability to exceed objectives, and work well with others.

**Personal Design Consultant** (1998 – 2000)
Recruited to assist homebuyers in selecting design options.
- Attained industry credentials as a Florida State Certified General Contractor and was immediately promoted.

FIVE BURROUGHS KITCHEN REMODELING CORP, Long Island, New York  1973 – 1998
**Owner**

Successfully managed full scope of daily operations including residential renovations; specialized in high-end custom kitchen installations, wholesale and retail.
- Operated as a Licensed Home Improvement Contractor, State of New York.

## CONTINUING DEVELOPMENT

- Centex Homes Customer First Training Program, 2000
- Pulte Corporate Code of Business Conduct and Ethics Training, 2006
- Pulte Heightened Awareness CPR Training, Earned Certification, 2006
- Numerous OSHA Training Course Certificates, University of South Florida

■■■■■

# CYNTHIA KATO, MBA

1234 Main Street, Miami, FL 33122
305-123-4567 (hm) • 305-123-6789 (mb)

**Global Systems & Operations**
Service • Telecom / IT • Finance

info@theresumestudio.com
*Open to relocation*

Results-driven **Senior Manager / Director-Level Operations Professional** with over 20 years of operations and systems experience. Dotted line management of up to 2,000 in-bound call center staff supporting four continents on behalf of Fortune 500 clients. Includes multi-lingual management across diverse cultures, languages and time zones in Asia, Australia, Europe, North America.

Operating and negotiating expertise with ability to drive vendor costs down while keeping productivity high and ensuring quality deliverables. Work well independently and in teams, mentoring direct managers and their reporting staff.

Described as swift but thorough, assertive yet understanding. Specialize in managing projects from definition and scope to oversight and delivery of on-time launch. Maximize capital through profitability improvements, cost reductions, excess elimination, and business model expansion. 100% commitment to meeting investor and customer expectations through low-price, high-yield solutions.

> *"Cynthia was key to the success of our core initiatives ... an asset to the team."*
>
> - **Jane Smyrl**
>   Sr. Director,
>   Customer Contact
>   Centers, Microsoft

**Languages**

- English
- Taiwanese
- Mandarin
- Tagalog

## AREAS OF EXPERTISE

- Account & Call Center Management
- SLA Compliance
- Planning, Implementation & Delivery
- Client / Customer Satisfaction Assurance
- Strategic Thinking & Problem Solving

- Vendor Relations & Negotiations
- Succession Planning
- Profitability & Accountability
- Systems & Operations
- Budgeting & Forecasting

## EXPERIENCE

**AllAccessCard** • Miami, FL                                                                 2005–present
*Providing credit building options to 40 million U.S. consumers otherwise turned away from credit opportunities.*

**Senior Manager, Implementation & Vendor Relations**, *7/06–present*
**Manager, Implementation & Vendor Relations**, *7/05–7/06*
**Manager, Implementation**, *2/05–7/05*
Hired and rapidly promoted as sole implementation project manager for mission-critical international projects including new card products (prepaid, gift card, pin based) and Web site overhaul. Awarded 20% salary increase within two months of hire for efficient, on-time / early project launches. Direct vendor negotiations and deal making (quote, shipping, inventory management). Liaison to banks and associations (Visa, MasterCard), and load partners (Western Union, MoneyGram, GreenDot, Visa/ReadyLink). Solely manage marketing content compliance. *Report to SVP, Marketing.*

- Struck "first in history of prepaid cards" deal with Western Union, providing free load to customer-based deposits of $300 and up. Launch date: May 2008
- Increased marketing collateral while decreasing postage costs by 30%, saving over $100k annually.
- Negotiated FedEx shipping costs down more than 50%.
- Managed 30+ launches in 12 months, the largest number of projects in one year since company inception.
- Launched prepaid Visa card program, now comprising 75% of monthly applications.

**Microsoft** (NasdaqGS: MSFT) • Seattle, WA                                2003–2005

*Leading desktop publishing software provider. FY06 revenues: $52B.*

### Senior Manager, Call Center Vendor Operations (NA, EMEA, APAC, and Japan)

Recruited to oversee all facets of outsourced worldwide technical and customer service vendors, while managing in-house FTEs and ensuring service agreement compliance. Liaised with vendors including Sykes, Supportandmore, Digital River, Modus, and Sutherland. Traveled internationally 35% of time. *Reported to Senior Director, Customer Contact Centers.*

- Reduced invoicing by 20% within 10 months.
- Salvaged outsourced vendor relationship within eight months of hire.
- Overhauled hiring and management practices of customer facing team; revised training protocols and materials.
- Performed front-end analysis for new outsource requirements including risk and compliance considerations, process and control reviews, and budget requirements.

**Convergys Corporation** (NYSE: CVG) • Cincinatti, OH / Tokyo, China                  1996–2003

*Forty technical help / customer support centers in the Americas, Asia, Africa and Europe. FY06 revenues: $2.9B.*

### Director, Client Services, 07/00–07/03
### General Manager, Operations | Convergys Asia Division, 03/96–08/00

Hired during period of vast growth to manage 2,000 seat, Tokyo-based, outsourced Tier I and II customer service and technology support call center. Managed operations and client services related to 24/7 multi-lingual provision of services on behalf of Adobe, Apple, Cisco, Citibank, Emerson, HP, Intel, Kodak, Macromedia, Microsoft,Motorola, Pegasus, Kodak, P&G, Redhat, SkyMall and U.S. Robotics.

Recruited internationally in 2000 to remotely lead U.S. operations. Provided global direction, planning, business analysis, performance review, and tactical recommendations. Acted as lead, advocate and trusted advisor to clients, assuring understanding of contractual relationships. Traveled 30% of time. *Dotted line supervision of seven senior account managers and 20 managers. Reported to VP and Managing Director, APAC.*

- Exceeded revenue growth by over 18% through personnel and process improvement.
- Increased annual revenues by $500,000 after expanding Cisco team by 200%.
- Salvaged $7.1 MM Macromedia account by underpinning contractual metrics.
- Generated 30% in cost savings through vendor negotiations.
- Expanded +/- 10,000% from 20-person start-up in 1996, to headcount of nearly 2,000 after by 2000.
- Held employee turnover rate to less than 5%, against 30% industry standard for competitive call centers.

*Early career (1990–1996) as regional and international systems engineer, consultant, and analyst for Kimoto Japan, Kimoto Thailand, and Thailand Alltrade, with work located in or focused on Japan, China, Thailand, and the U.S.*

## PROFILE

Shanghai Jiao Tong University, Shanghai, China

**MBA,** *1992* • Dean's List
**BAC, Accounting,** *1990* • Dean's List

Technology: Fluent in MS Word, Excel,
PowerPoint, and Outlook; and the Internet

**Awards & Accomplishments**
Best in Team, *1993*
Kimoto Japan, Osaka, Japan

- *First woman assigned to corporate headquarters.*

# MICHAEL LANGSTON

3874 Duchess Trail • Plano, Texas 75035 • mlangston@sbcglobal.net • (214) 653-8994

---

## SALES MANAGER / BUSINESS DEVELOPMENT MANAGER
### Expertise In: Semiconductor, Chemical, and Solar Energy Industries

*"Consistently exceed revenue and margin targets by providing strategic account management, penetrating new markets, building strong and lasting relationships with decision-makers, and maintaining excellent communication with customers to ensure retention."*

**Former engineer offering 13+ years' of proven experience growing global and domestic sales revenue, managing key accounts, and providing decisive account leadership in technical industries.**

Superior interpersonal skills that foster ability to interact effectively with a variety of internal departments to support sales, marketing, and customer retention goals. Known for ability to work well and communicate capably with engineers and high-level executives. Recognized for perfect customer retention. History of success addressing and overcoming routine challenges in the areas of manufacturing, quality, and delivery. Computer proficiencies include Word, Excel, PowerPoint, and SAP.

### Core Sales Competencies:

- Prospecting / Cold Calling
- Activity Reporting / Forecasting
- Rapport Building
- Revenue Growing
- Consultative Selling
- Negotiating / Closing
- New Hire Training
- Retaining Customers
- Problem Solving

## PROFESSIONAL EXPERIENCE

CAPA Electronic Materials, Inc., Jefferson, Missouri                                       1995–2008

*~ Publically traded, global company that manufacturers high-purity silicon wafers and polysilicon used to manufacture semiconductors and photovoltaics. Company generated about $2 billion in revenue in 2007. ~*

**GLOBAL ACCOUNT MANAGER,** Denison, Texas (2002–2008)

Promoted to manage global business-to-business sales and coordinate activities in marketing, scheduling, application engineering, manufacturing, and quality control to support business and revenue objectives. Traveled domestically 20% of time and internationally to Europe once a year.

Sold globally to Freescale (formerly Motorola) and Spansion (formerly part of AMD). Sold silicon wafers in the U.S. to company's "Top Two" customers—Samsung and STMicroelectronics. Functioned as Account Manager for Sematech, Atmel, Microchip, and ON Semiconductor.

- **SALES VOLUME / REVENUE GROWTH:**
  - **Consistently generated sales in excess of $30 million annually,** beyond revenue target goals and ahead of average company growth rate.
  - **Drove sales 500% to ON Semiconductor** after becoming qualified on a new product.
  - **Expanded Motorola revenues 228%**—from $3.5 million/quarter in 2004 to $8 million/quarter in 2008.
  - **Increased revenue 200% at Spansion** the first year on account.
  - **Grew revenue 15% from STMicroelectronics** over two quarters to $3.4 million/quarter.
- **MARKET SHARE:**
  - **Grew market share 200% at Spansion** the first year on account.
  - **Increased market share 20% at Motorola in Europe**—from 5% to 25% by negotiating competitive pricing, building strong relationships with decision makers, and providing quality customer service.
  - **Maintained "Number One" market share** at STMicroelectronics.
- **KEY SUPPLIER STATUS: Continuously maintained key-supplier status at Samsung.** Recently secured approval to introduce CAPA's next-generation wafer for qualification.
- **HONORS: Twice recognized with "Supplier Performance Award"—in 2006 from Freescale and in 2005 from AMD**—for being the top supplier in wafer division.

*... Continued ...*

## PROFESSIONAL EXPERIENCE (CONTINUED)

**MARKETING MANAGER,** Pasadena, Texas (1995–2002)

Recruited from Raleigh Corporation to manage the marketing/sales department for CAPA's polysilicon plant, formulate marketing plan and individual account strategies, supervise department employees, set department budget and goals, forecast sales, and negotiate contracts.

Coordinated activities of technology, manufacturing, and quality-assurance departments to support marketing goals. Position entailed 40% domestic travel and quarterly overseas travel. Reported directly to President, CAPA Pasadena, with dotted-line responsibility to Corporate VP of Sales

- **SALES VOLUME / REVENUE GROWTH:**
  - — **Drove unprecedented revenue growth—163% in two years—**from $33 million to $54 million. Mostly attributed to diversification strategy of polysilicon into solar energy.
  - — **Grew silane sales 60% in 2000 and another 30% in 2001.**
  - — **Maxed out sales of polysilicon from 1995–1997.** Plant could not produce enough to keep up with sales and that's what led to $26 million-dollar plant expansion.
  - — **Maxed out sales of by-products.** Kept them sold-out for entire tenure.
- **DIVERSIFICATION STRATEGY:**
  - — **Led plant sales activities through a complete cycle in semiconductor industry** and developed strategy to diversify into solar energy market. Solar energy now represents CAPA's fastest-growing business segment.
  - — **Company achieved status as one of the "Top Three" polysilicon suppliers** in solar energy by 2000.
- **BUSINESS EXPANSION:**
  - — **Recognized for reversing downward trend in market share** of silane gas by formulating and implementing innovative business expansion.
  - — **Played a key role in recommending $26 million-dollar plant expansion** that was realized in 1998.
  - — **Successfully penetrated Japan, Korean, and Taiwan markets.**
  - — **Realized Asian expansion by lowering product costs and enabling competitive pricing** by developing plans to build a new manifold and changing packaging into bulk containers.
  - — **Secured approval of $1.2 million capital investment** in project from top management.
- **CONTRACT NEGOTIATION:**
  - — **Spearheaded lucrative contract negotiation** to sell industrial gas in a new market.
  - — **Recognized for negotiating first contract** in which Japanese customers were buying from non-Japanese suppliers.

**PREVIOUS EMPLOYMENT INCLUDES:**

Raleigh Corporation, Raleigh, North Carolina

**PRODUCT SUPERVISOR/MANAGER** (acted as Account Manager at CAPA Electronic Materials, Inc.)
**SENIOR R&D ENGINEEER,** (supervised four R&D engineers)

## EDUCATION, DEVELOPMENT & PROFESSIONAL AFFILIATIONS

**MASTER OF CHEMICAL ENGINEERING,** University of Houston

**BACHELOR OF SCIENCE, PETROLEUM ENGINEERING,** Pennsylvania State University, University Park

**CERTIFICATE OF COMPLETION, WORLD CLASS BUSINESS PRACTICES,** Washington University, John M. Olin School of Business, St. Louis, Missouri

**MEMBER,** Society of Chemical Engineers

• • • • •

# KELLY LOWE

5 Ives Dairy Road, 11F
Boston, MA 33139

Phone: 305-889-9632
kelly@krown.com

## Fashion Designer with 10+ years of expertise in creative fabric development

### BIO BITS

- ❖ **Business Management:** Evolved knitting thesis into one-of-a-kind showcase studio of creative signature fabric and unique yarn and garment combinations.
- ❖ **Fashion and Textile Design:** Draft, develop and produce unique fabric and garment designs.
- ❖ **Financial Performance:** Achieve profits of +$300K in 3-year period; +40% growth each year.
- ❖ **Communications Strategy:** Participate in ad campaigns; gain exposure through features in international media and tradeshows, fashion shows, performances and gallery showings.

### CAREER HIGHLIGHTS

- ❖ Founder of successful knitting and garment production line. Recognized for designs in over 100 fashion shows, trade shows, ad campaigns, performance and gallery showings, boutiques, dance and theater productions. Modeled by celebrity clients, such as **Alanis Morissette, Christina Ricci, Fergie, Cameron Diaz, Hilary Duff, Courtney Love, Pink,** among others.
- ❖ Designed woven fabric patterns purchased by Dim underwear label for undergarment and T-shirt production in France (1996).
- ❖ Incorporated high-end fashion manufacturing business; oversee essential business fundamentals and continue to strategize knitting design and garment production.
- ❖ Conducted guest Lecture at Parsons The New School for Design: Guest Lecture "Starting your career in school" for 20 photographers (2006).
- ❖ Lectured on knitting collection at Rhode Island School of Design for a textile class of 25 (2001).

### FASHION KEY POINTS

| | | |
|---|---|---|
| Unique Fabric Design | Flat Bed Machine and Woven Knits | Pret-a-Porter Fashion |
| Weaving Drafting | Industrial Machine Knitting | Multi-Harness Loom |
| Manufacturing Strategy | Advanced English/French Skills | Jacquard Design |

### FASHION MANAGEMENT EXPERIENCE

**Kellycreate, Inc.,** Boston, MA .................................................................2002 - present
**Administrator - Designer**
Incorporated business after first year due to successful take-off. Design and produce pret-a-porter collections of women's contemporary knitwear. Supervise team of three employees. Direct hand and industrial machine knitting manufacturing process. Organize fashion shows, lectures, sales presentations, and wholesale management to boutiques.

- Featured as a designer and fashion manager in 50+ articles, editorials, and TV segments.
- Invited to participate in internationally acclaimed trade shows in New York, LA, London, Miami.
- Chosen as a Gen Art Fresh Face in Fashion one year after line was launched (2003).
- Selected to appear with designs in two international advertising campaigns.
- Competed in the Perrier Bubbling Under Fashion Show at Funkshion Fashion Week in Miami, resulting in self-produced shows for Fall 2006/Spring 2007 collections.
- Invited to present collections in 15 renowned Fashion Shows, such as Los Angeles Fashion Week, Miami Fashion Week, and Berlin Fashion Week, among other special events.

**Christian Dior, Rodeo Drive Shops,** Boston, MA ............................................................... 1997 - 1999
**Store Manager**
Performed sales, merchandise tracking, customer service, and in charge of opening and closing store.
- Managed start-up operations and sales for high-end garments surpassing sales goals in one year.
- Supervised four employees on sales of Christian Dior brand.
- Tracked daily sales log and conducted inventory checks.

**Escada,** Paris, France ............................................................................................................. 1996
**Design Assistant, Textile Design**
Designed patterns for printed and woven fabrics, ready-to-wear, haute couture, and lingerie. Final pattern designs were put into production.
- Created repeat pattern designs selected by upscale labels for garment manufacturing.

### OTHER FASHION EXPERIENCE

**Lion Theater Company,** Boston, MA ...................................................................... 2000 - 2006
**Costume Designer**
Purchased and created a look for the actors in each play performed:
- Head costume designer for six seasons.
- Selected to conduct a Performing Arts Workshop for 15 students.
- Produced and and co-directed two night shows.

**Design and Architecture Senior High School,** Boston, MA ............................... 2004 - 2005
**Adjunct Professor of Textile Hand Techniques**

**The Field,** Boston, MA ............................................................................................ 2001 - 2002
**Facilitator of Performance Workshops**

**South Light Project,** Boston, MA ......................................................................... 2000 - 2002
**Arts Administrator**
Conducted accounting, ticket sales, bookkeeping, and public relations.

**Boston Grand Opera,** Boston, MA ........................................................................ 1998 - 1999
**Costume Design Apprentice**

**Freelance Costume Designer** [several theater and dance companies], Boston, MA ............ 1997 - 2006

### EDUCATION

**Rhode Island School of Design,** Providence, RI ................................................. 1995 - 1997
**BFA 1997, Textiles Design**

**Bragallen,** Stockholm, Sweden .............................................................................. 1993
**Textiles Summer Program**

### SKILLS AND INTERESTS

- Skills in Graphic Design, Industrial and Hand Knitting Machine Techniques, Knitting Production, Industrial Machine Sewing, Pattern making, Weaving, Surface Design.
- Excellent communication skills in English and French, basic Spanish.
- Advance computer skills in Adobe Illustrator, Photoshop CS 7.0, MS Office Suite (Word, Excel, and PowerPoint), Internet Navigation Tools.

# Jon Lugent, RN, MBA

119002 Sharpe Drive, San Jose, CA 94122

Cell: (408) 209-7922 / jlugent2323@aol.com

### HEALTHCARE OPERATIONS
### MANAGEMENT & CONSULTING

*Innovative business management professional with 10-year career in healthcare and hospital management prefaced with 5 years of experience as a Registered Nurse in multiple medical facilities. Expertise reaches into operations management and systems management as well as marketing and business development.*

> ➤ Ability to integrate principles of business, finance, and human resources while maintaining accountability to organizational policies and accreditation standards as they relate to patient care.

> ➤ In-depth knowledge of hospital operations spanning administration, admissions, legal, laboratory, pharmacy, triage, intensive care, and ER – due to experience as RN, ANO, EMT, and Staffing Specialist.

> ➤ Collaboration with all levels of staff and executive leadership from the Bay Area's diverse medical centers.

> ➤ Talent for recruiting, training, developing, and managing clinical staff and sales/marketing personnel.

---

### MANAGEMENT EXPERIENCE

---

**Director of Branch Operations: Medical Staffing, Inc., Palo Alto, CA**          **20xx to Present**

Assumed leadership over understaffed 4-year old branch challenged with stagnant $8 million annual revenue. Across 5 years, more than doubled branch headcount, solidified existing client relationships, and acquired new accounts with leading medical organizations throughout the Bay Area, boosting revenues 150% and bringing San Jose Branch from #6 corporate position to #2 (second only to long standing northwest tri-state territory).

#### Client Management & Strategic Relationships

- Established and retained strategic relationships with executive-level nursing leads at San Francisco General, UCSF, Summit Alta Bates, Marin General, Kaiser Permanente, St. Francis, St. Mary's, Valley Care, and San Ramon Regional to address clinical and interpersonal matters.

- Supported dramatic 300%-400% revenue increases at high-volume Bay Area hospitals, Alta Bates ($1.9 million in 20xx) and San Francisco General ($2.5 million in 20xx), by serving as preferred agent for 4 years.

- Generated $1 million per annum in new business (University of Pacific, Marin General, Sequoia Surgical).

#### Staff Leadership & Infrastructure Development

- Groomed 9 new recruits into seasoned recruiters in the span of 3 years by providing 3-6 month initial trainings plus subsequent shadowing, reverse shadowing, and hands-on sales coaching.

- Developed new program resulting in a 25% increase in bill rates by lengthening weekly shifts from 36 hours to 48 hours. This initiative attracted more on-call nurses, enabling Medical Staffing, Inc. to meet more clients' needs at a lower cost not only to the client but also to Medical Staffing, Inc.

- Reduced a/r turnaround time by almost 50% (from 80 days to 46 days sales outstanding).

---

**Administrative Nursing Officer: San Francisco General Hospital, San Francisco, CA**          **20xx to 20xx**

Oversaw graveyard shift comprised of 75-100 nurses and clerical staff for this 571-bed, inner-city private hospital. Provided both nursing and ad-hoc management consulting services, taking the lead in streamlining creating distribution lists, developing order systems, and compiling and organizing voluminous vendor archives.

#### Staff Leadership & Direction

- Earned recognition as executive decision maker for all fiscal, clinical, and administrative matters by nurses, technicians, lab specialists, and pharmacists.

- Served additional role as the travel nurse coordinator to hire, process, and orient travel and registered nurses sourced out of national staffing firms and local per diem registries.

## CLINICAL NURSING EXPERIENCE

| | |
|---|---|
| Traveling Registered Nurse, Emergency Department: Various Employers (see list below) | 19xx to 20xx |
| Registered Nurse / Emergency Department Staff Nurse: University of Chicago Hospitals | 19xx to 19xx |

| | |
|---|---|
| Medical Staffing, Inc. | San Jose, CA; Fairfield, CA |
| Nursing Leaders | Charlotte, NC; Nashville, TN |
| U.S. Quality Nurses | St. Thomas, USVI; Vancouver, BC; Boulder, CO (Charge RN) |
| QRS Healthcare | Boston, MA; Grand Rapids, MI; Reno, NV (Trauma L-2) |
| Warton International | South Lake Tahoe, CA (Ski Patrol RN) |
| University of Nevada Hospitals | Reno, NV (Pediatric Trauma L-1) |

## VOLUNTEER HEALTHCARE WORK

| | |
|---|---|
| EMT / Firefighter / Health Education Instructor: Woskee Township, Woskee, TN | 19xx to 20xx |

Championed *First Responder Program* for Woskee Township Fire Department including serving as lead medical officer over volunteer EMTs and First Responders.

### Health Education Training
- Taught cardiopulmonary resuscitation, first aid, and HIV curriculum to students ranging in age and experience from preschoolers to industrial engineers.

## EDUCATION AND AFFILIATIONS

**Executive MBA, University of Santa Clara School of Management, CA**      **20xx**
Graduated beta gamma sigma (top 10% of class) for this 15-month intensive business program.
Won Western Medical Leaders scholarship awarded to business-minded scholars who've excelled in Nursing.

**ACNL Member (Association of California Nurse Leaders)**      **Since 19xx**
Patient Care Committee, Santa Clara Chapter      Since 20xx
Urgent Care Committee, San Jose Chapter      Since 20xx

**BS Nursing, Tenessee University School of Nursing, Nashville, TN**      **19xx**

# Jon Lugent, RN, MBA

Cell: (408) 209-7922 / jlugent2323@aol.com

# AUDREY MACDONALD

audreym@hotmail.com

32895 Hardison Place, NE
Washington, DC 20019

Residence: 202-659-1255
Cellular: 202-675-6137

## SENIOR MARKETING EXECUTIVE
### Accessories – Intimate Apparel – Luxury Brands – Beauty Products

#### SEALING THE PRODUCT'S BRAND INTO THE HEARTS OF CONSUMERS
*Orchestrating integrated, multimedia marketing communication campaigns that propel brand awareness, accelerate customer traffic, secure customer loyalty, and increase bottom-line sales*

##### BRAND AWARENESS • CONSUMER PERCEPTION • SALES, REVENUE & PROFIT GROWTH

Pioneering, strategic thinking executive with dynamic record of delivering marketing solutions that transform interested consumers into loyal customers. Consistently introduced new, "first-of-its-kind" marketing and advertising concepts that resulted in product differentiation and competitive advantage for leading retailers.

## —MARKETING MANAGEMENT EXPERIENCE & PERFORMANCE HIGHLIGHTS—

| SENIOR VICE PRESIDENT – MARKETING AND ADVERTISING, **LADY SOLES INTERNATIONAL, INC** | 2006 to present |
|---|---|

Brought onboard to re-position and re-brand products suffering from declining sales due to increased industry competition. Restructured traditional advertising and direct marketing programs to support integrated marketing strategies including direct mail, e-commerce, in-store visuals, and trade show exhibitions. Managed $25 million budget and staff of nine employees.

- **Public & Media Relations:** Attracted premium coverage in high-profile media outlets like USA Today, the Today Show, Oprah Magazine, and Lucky Magazine.

- **Online Product Promotions:** Drove significant surge in online product sales by directing the content development and re-launch of Ladysoles.com.

| VICE PRESIDENT – MARKETING AND ADVERTISING, **MARKETING BRANDS, INC.** | 2003 to 2006 |
|---|---|

Recruited to develop and execute comprehensive marketing strategy for company's top-selling product during a period of accelerated growth. Charged with instituting advertising, branding, and communication initiatives to build product awareness, increase customer loyalty, and expand market share. Managed $10 million budget, 20 employees, and contracts with advertising/public relations agencies.

- **Revenue Growth:** Championed the development of marketing and product promotion techniques that doubled annual revenues in just three years.

- **Corporate Branding:** Engineered a corporate-wide, re-branding plan for product differentiation and identification. Revamped all corporate marketing materials and collateral including company logo, building signs, business cards, and shopping bags.

- **Corporate Communications:** Garnered employee buy-in by introducing bi-monthly corporate newsletter that celebrated employees' successes and increased peer-to-peer collaboration.

- **New Product Marketing:** Conceived the largest new product launch in 20 years by assembling fully integrated marketing program with department stores – from direct mail, store displays, sales events, and special promotions.
  - Organized international marketing campaigns in Europe, South America, and Asia.

- **Public Relations:** Doubled product exposure in leading fashion magazines—including a featured editorial in the New York Times business section—by commencing highly targeted public relation events.

**BROOKS BROTHERS CORPORATION**                                           1990 to 2002

*Rapid career progression through increasingly challenging roles in brand and advertising campaign management, global product marketing, and multimedia marketing communications. Repeatedly instituted strategies that drove annual sales, promoted brand awareness, and increased product recognition. Representative positions:*

---

VICE PRESIDENT – MENSWEAR MARKETING (2001 to 2002)

---

Selected to implement new marketing strategies and ignite sales growth for the top brands in menswear department. Restored existing business relationships with national retailers to confer on cooperative advertising efforts, sales promotions, and special events. Managed $30 million budget and supervised up to 25 employees.

- **Multimedia Marketing Communications:** Drove sales on featured product 15% by pioneering a retail marketing program during the Father's Day shopping period for the time in company's history.
  - Devised full scope of marketing, advertising, and branding initiatives encompassing direct mail, newspaper placements, in-store visuals, and charity special events.
- **Strategic Partnerships:** Delivered 40% increased sell-thru on featured product sales by forging media partnership between company and *GQ Magazine*.

---

VICE PRESIDENT – LICENSEE MARKETING (1997 to 2001)

---

Challenged to originate multifaceted, luxury brand marketing program for international affiliates in London, Paris, Hong Kong, Tokyo, Sydney, Chile, and Buenos Aires. Tasked with creating marketing materials for in-store advertising, media, and public relation programs and identifying the right product mix for international consumers.

- **Global / International Marketing:** Spearheaded, coordinated, and hosted the company's first "*International Marketing Conference*" to educate global marketing executives on the company brand, forge viable working relationships, and collaborate on standard marketing guidelines.
- **Strategic Market Plans:** Orchestrated store opening plans for seven freestanding locations and developed international marketing campaigns for 75 shop-in-shop concepts.
- **Competitive Product Positioning:** Revitalized brand awareness and peaked consumer interest by developing shop-in-shop retail concepts, increasing media exposure opportunities, and coordinating high-profile special events.

---

DIRECTOR – RETAIL ADVERTISING (1993 to 1997)
MANAGER (1990 to 1993)

---

Promoted to manage advertising and product branding programs for nationwide retail stores. Liaised between retail stores and corporate marketing department to ensure consistency in product promotions and advertisements.

- **Product Promotions:** Gave company access to $1.8 million in value-added programs by strategically negotiating magazine advertising.
- **Product Branding:** Increased product sales 25% and generated subsequent increases between 15% to 40% by launching special advertising incentives with retail partners at flagship locations.

—**EDUCATION**—

BS, Marketing and Communications – Fashion Institute of Technology, SUNY

# WILLA SANDY MERRICK

555 Thatcher Avenue, Jersey City, NJ 07305
cell: 212.904.3377, willamerrickr@msn.com

*Ambitious, energetic entry- to mid-level business professional with classroom training and real-world experience in marketing, market research, market analysis & reporting, and production. Strong long-term interest in international business as demonstrated by volunteer activities, student organization leadership, and cultural studies abroad.*

| | | |
|---|---|---|
| EDUCATION | **STATE UNIVERSITY OF NEW YORK, BUFFALO, NEW YORK** | **20xx** |
| | *Bachelor of Science in Business Administration,* School of Business | |

STUDENT
LEADERSHIP

*Director of Marketing, Roteract Club (20xx-20xx)*
Led marketing efforts for two consecutive years to develop and promote this college division of Rotery International comprised of 75 business-minded students. Spearheaded "R you in?" campaign, using Roteract brand to reach 1000+ undergraduates. Planned and designed fliers, posters, and T-shirts.

*Business Policy & Ethics Project (20xx)*
Applied business techniques to real-world client, Ross Pharmaceuticals in order to draft 1500-page 2-volume handbook detailing existing policies and recommended improvements. As part of team, researched Ross' annual report, evaluated strategy, performed analyses, and discussed ethical issues.

*Service Leadership Project (20xx)*
Examined means of reducing overhead for up-state cancer wellness center across a three-month period, eventually cutting costs 50% on annual fundraising event via logistics restructuring.

*Principles of Marketing Planning Committee (20xx)*
Designed marketing plan for a local sports correction athletic company.

INTERNSHIPS
(3-MONTHS)

*Marketing Assistant, Amuck (D&C Traders) (20xx)*
Assisted the Design and Marketing Managers by providing administrative support and marketing services for this leading sandal manufacturing company. Assembled and delivered art samples to national magazines, performed trend analysis, and sat in on marketing meetings alongside design, graphics, and production staff.

*Finance Assistant, Smith Barney Citigroup (20xx)*
Took up an administrative position in Finance to explore business from an angle outside of Marketing. Attended meetings with Smith Barney partners and clients with a focus on retirement plans, stocks and bond investing, real estate investment, and other investment options.

INTERNATIONAL
COMMUNITY
INVOLVEMENT

*"Semester At Sea" via University of Pennsylvania at Pittsburgh (20xx)*
Participated in "Semester at Sea" program, touring the Pacific Rim to study the language, culture, and business practices in Canada, Russia, Japan, Australia, New Zealand, and Fiji. Coursework included international negotiations, world geography, world history, language studies, and art history.

*Roteract Club (20xx-20xx)*
Organized several domestic and international projects: tutored elementary school students, planned community cleanup day, and coordinated trips to holiday events for orphanages in Mexico.

*Habitat for Humanity (20xx)*
Assisted in the construction of 2-story Habitat for Humanity house in Buffalo County. Placed in charge of securing funds and support from local churches.

*Volunteer Activities (1999, 20xx, 20xx-20xx)*
Taught English to orphans in Mexico (20xx-20xx), visited an orphanage in the Ukraine (20xx), and helped build lodging to teach children English and Math in Costa Rica (19xx).

| **EMPLOYMENT** | ***Research Analyst, Alfa Developers, Inc., Bayonne, NJ*** | ***2006-current; 20xx-20xx*** |
| --- | --- | --- |

Initially hired into part-time administrative position to learn business procedures within the commercial and residential real estate market while obtaining business degree. Upon graduation, assumed full-time role focused on market research and analysis.

- Currently performing preliminary research for residential/retail/industrial development projects to determine buyer demographic and market value for potential sites. Remain in contact with city planners to ascertain development wish list and flesh out opportunities.
- Assembled 50-page report on research findings including website printouts, onsite photos, and detailed analysis and recommendations.
- Attended strategy meetings to listen in on discussions over land use, engineering issues, site plans, general plans, budget, performa data, and city council intervention.
- Provided administrative services such as archiving receipts and legal documents and reviewing loan documents, contracts, and planning department applications.

***Project Manager, White Dove Development, Buffalo, NY***      ***20xx-20xx***

Assumed full responsibility for the bidding, negotiation, and execution of all contracts as well as the site management for the design and construction of two custom homes reaching 3,000 to 7,000 square feet. Eventually left this position to return to New Jersey.

- Coordinated and enforced the work schedules of 20 contractors, juggling logistics of up to six onsite contractors daily. Arranged for delivery of building materials as needed.
- Utilized phone and fax to communicate with laborers, serving as the only in-house Spanish-speaking employee.
- Assisted supervisor with design and production activities such as retrieving and consolidating paint/fabric samples.
- Troubleshot unforeseen weather stripping complications such as leaking windows and doors. Assessed problem, devised strategy, and reassigned contractors as needed.

| **TECHNICAL PROFICIENCY** | Mac and Windows operating systems: Microsoft Office (Word, Excel, PowerPoint), basic Access database experience. Conversational Spanish. |
| --- | --- |

| **INTERESTS** | Extremely competitive and active in snowboarding, tennis, running, swimming, skating, and scuba diving. Trained with three tennis coaches, including Rob Stanley, a local tennis pro. Former member of SUNY's snowboarding club (20xx-20xx) and a big fan of winter and summer outdoor team sports. |
| --- | --- |

Member and Panhellenic Chair of Executive Board for Pi Beta Phi (ΠΒΦ) sorority (20xx-20xx).

*Portfolio of press releases, marcom pieces, and design samples available upon request*

# BARRY MORGAN, CPA

1650 Wilkes Street • Jersey City, NJ 07302 • H: 201-268-0655 • C: 201-982-1202 • bmorgan@gmail.com

## FINANCIAL MANAGEMENT EXECUTIVE

Start-Ups • Turnarounds • Workouts • Process Improvement • Multi-Unit Retail

Diverse senior accounting professional with experience in public, private, government, and not-for-profit environments. Solid track record of achievement managing multimillion-dollar M&A activity, establishing and running company subsidiaries, and implementing change technology and methods to reorganize, streamline, and strengthen financial operations and maximize performance, profitability, and opportunity. Apply exceptional integrity and comprehensive expertise in financial reporting and analysis, forecasting, budgeting, cash management, auditing, and controls.

## CORE COMPETENCIES

Senior Financial Management • Private Equity Finance/Operations • M&A Due Diligence • Change Management • IT Planning/Conversion • SEC Reporting • Public Accounting • Bankruptcy/Receivership Workout • Contract Negotiations
SAP • SunGard Trust Accounting • Quickbooks Enterprise Solutions • MS Office

## PROFESSIONAL EXPERIENCE

**HAAS & LOWELL CAPITAL, L.L.C.,** JERSEY CITY, NJ                                    2001 to Present

*Private equity firm managing technology, retail, transportation, and real estate companies.*

**Controller and Partner -** Established/led accounting function to improve operations management, internal control, point-of-sale reporting integrity/uniformity, back-office efficiency, and key metrics reporting.

*M&A Activity*

- **Reversed previously failed acquisition bid and successfully led $17.5M sale** of privately held software company to NYSE-listed buyer by reengineering revenue recognition, restating financial results and spearheading M&A financial due diligence. Appointed CFO and Director of company.

- **Developed business case, detailed projections, and industry/competitor information** for additional M&A activity including new business with nationwide market.

*Financial Growth (for multi-site retailer)*

- **Doubled gross margin (from 20% to 40%),** gained greater visibility and control over quality and turnover by converting retail merchandise inventory from manual records to electronic scanning, tracking, and reporting.

- **Realized profitability gains of $155,000 in one year** while boosting individual accountability and manager retention by establishing inaugural manager incentive bonus program based on overall site profitability.

*Cost Savings and Process Improvements (for multi-site retailer)*

- **Cut excess wage payments by 15% and trimmed non-critical expenses on average 8%** across the board for 8 operations; improved budgeting/forecasting capabilities exponentially by restructuring financial statement line items to provide more detail, clarity, visibility, and consistency in revenue and expense line items.

- **Unlocked $290,000 in savings** and increased manager accountability by imbedding hourly productivity metric into weekly management reporting and budgeting.

- **Slashed time troubleshooting site operating system issues in half** (from 6 hours to 3 hours or less) by establishing in-house support versus long-distance telephone support model. The same model also **reduced software conversion support costs by 75%** while conforming menu offerings to uniform formats.

**BLAIRE FOUNDATION OF NEW JERSEY,** JERSEY CITY, NJ                                    1996 to 2000

*Not-for-profit financial services institution with $2B in assets.*

**Vice President/Controller,** Cord Trust Company subsidiary (1996 to 2000) - Established for-profit, regulated trust company to offer financial services constituent clients. Created/led accounting function and installed infrastructure allowing **account growth to $275M (1,200 accounts) in 3 years.** Board level reporting responsibility.

**Director of Operations** (1998 to 1999) – Recruited by CEO to project manage a $1.5M 15-month financial systems conversion and process improvement project; directed needs assessment and vendor selection process, negotiated software/hardware contracts, and led organization through live processing. Managed staff of 9.

- Mitigated risk associated with antiquated accounting system by transitioning system maintenance and support to a proven third-party with NYSE profile. **Negotiated a 25% discount off software/services contract.**

- **Reduced manpower needed to rebalance investment accounts by 40%** (from 5 to 3 people), cut fiduciary tax preparation staff in half, eliminated manual input/human error in securities pricing, and elevated standards for donor and beneficiary reporting by introducing robust reporting features and new electronic interfaces.

- Increased internal control and efficiency by centralizing all trust endowment and related investment security processing and settlement functions into one department with uniform procedures.

**AMBLE SYSTEMS, INC.,** HOBOKEN, NJ                                       1995 to 1996

*Privately owned software company catering to niche market of large banks and Bank Secrecy Act (BSA) compliance.*

**Regional Marketing Manager**

- Closed over 90% of prospects and captured close to a million dollars in sales in 18 months. 75% of first year's sales production included licensing relationships to the U.S. "Top 25" banks.

**FEDERAL INSURANCE CORPORATION,** JERSEY CITY, NJ                          1991 to 1995

*Federal agency charged with oversight/work-out of loans from failed banks.*

**Financial Oversight Accountant -** Provided financial management support to oversight board in its decision-making role managing and disposing of asset pools ranging from $700M to $4.4B acquired from failed financial institutions. Resolved national contract issues among contractors and FDIC accounting units, facilitated dispute resolution, and coordinated internal/external audit fieldwork.

- **Recouped $6.6M for agency** and received Sustained Performance Special Achievement Award for successfully managing contracts/contractor relationships.

**FIRST TRUST BANK CORPORATION,** DEBTOR-IN-POSSESSION, NEWARK, NJ            1985 to 1990

**Vice President and Chief Accounting Officer** (1988 to 1990) - Recruited to become CAO to oversee company's bankruptcy proceedings. Managed $500M cash and securities, and tax, accounting, and reporting functions. Prepared consolidated SEC (10K, 10Q) and court filings. Extensive involvement in analysis and due diligence for asset dispositions, development of reorganization plans, litigation support, and bankruptcy claims resolution. Supervised staffs of up to 15 employees and outside professionals.

- Secured company's right to approximately $60M in value by planning and participating in offensive/defensive measures to protect assets from third-party interests. Negotiated sale of leasehold interest in airplane facility for 105% of appraised value.

**Manager, Parent/Non Bank Subsidiaries Accounting** (1987 to 1988)        **Internal Audit Supervisor** (1985 to 1987)

- Performed consolidations of first, second, and third-tier subsidiaries, encompassing close to 75 entities. Avoided early non-monetary defaults by re-establishing compliance with debt covenant reporting requirements for five publicly held senior and subordinated debt issues.

- Planned/executed audits of major functions in banks ranging from $200M to $15B in assets.

### CONTRACTING WORK

Bing & Lewis, Inc (9/00 to 6/01) • Trust America Corporation Contractors (1/91 to 6/91)

### EARLY CAREER

Glibb & Blair, a national accounting firm, Audit Supervisor, Audit Senior, Staff Accountant (1981 to 1985) and Ebbs, Smith & Co., a regional accounting firm, Staff Accountant (1980 to 1981)

### EDUCATION, PROFESSIONAL LICENSES, AND AFFILIATIONS

Certified Public Accountant, 1983 • B.B.A., Accounting, Rutgers University, 1980

Member, American Institute of Certified Public Accountants

## Mark S. Paladino
*Non-stop, nothing-is-impossible leader and pacesetter*

555-555-1111 Mobile • markp@emailme.net
15 Center Street • Phoenix, AZ 44877

### Global Manufacturing Quality Assurance and Production Management

Six Sigma Green Belt ~ Continuous Process Improvement ~ Lean Manufacturing ~ ISO Certifications
SAP Power User ~ SPC Implementation ~ Customer Service Quality Improvement

| AREAS OF EXPERTISE | VALUE |
|---|---|
| New Part Qualification<br>New Product Development<br>Vendor Qualifying & Partnering<br>Root Cause Analysis<br>Design to Cost<br>1$^{st}$ Article Inspections<br>Process Capability Studies<br>Corrective Action Investigations<br>CMM Inspection<br>Tracking QR Activity (SAS)<br>Equipment Effectiveness<br>Manual Assembly<br>Metallurgical Requirements | Relentless fixer, turning around and revitalizing underproductive processes, benchmarking quality manufacturing practices, and driving top-performance from cross-cultural teams in China, Europe, Mexico, and the U.S.<br><br>*Routinely propel triple-digit cost reductions and increase throughput against impossible odds.*<br><br>Staying-power to get the best out of cross-divisional teams (production, engineering, and maintenance) by involving them from the ground floor. Firm believer in earning and reciprocating respect.<br><br>*No-boundaries approach to quality and reliability improvement, persistently exposing and correcting defective products and internal defects. A valued advisor with unwavering integrity.* |

### Manufacturing Management – Experience and Achievements

CRYSTAL LIGHTING, Phoenix, AL
$5.5 billion global leader in recessed and fluorescent lighting manufacture.

2003 to Present

*Led Six Sigma (MVP) imperatives capturing $293K annual cost reduction.*
*Drove cross-divisional team to $285K reduction in 2006 facility warranty costs.*

**Quality Manager, Incandescent Operations**
Troubleshoot and liaise daily with Crystal's 3 facilities in Mexico and several suppliers in China. Benchmarked procedures to qualify new vendors – PPAP, APQP, Process Capability, SPC Study, 8D, FMEA, 1$^{st}$ Article Inspection. Maintained and tweaked ISO certification procedures. Hold full P&L responsibility for $2mm capital budget and $200K operating budget. Ground-floor contributor to SAP Implementation process.

- Reduced by 50% defective product rejections for lighting reflectors by rewriting visual specifications and introducing in-house training at Crystal and end supplier.
- Saved estimated $40K in warranty costs with one shot fix, expediting correction and retool of defective part from China.
- Saved estimated $500K in warranty costs kicking off Lumiere and Metalux product redesign to resolve perennial field complaints and reduce high volume of warranty claims.
- Reduced annualized warranty cost $250K by designing tox gage using static weight test correlating to tox-loc X dimension. Eliminated need to send to lab for pull strength test.
- Saved $28K with decision to scrap instead of rework product with misleading label information, resolving 3-year standing problem.

AEROSPACE ENGINEERING INTERNATIONAL, INC., Montgomery, AL
(Division of Pratt & Whitney)

1998 to 2003

*Drove measurable advances expediting processes – captured double-digit annual savings,*
*reduced development time, enhanced flexibility, and improved customer service quality.*

**Quality Manager (2000-2003)**
Co-wrote ISO and AS 9100 procedures and facilitated training. Generated quality system tracking for new ERP system. Developed 4 part numbers for Rolls-Royce and 12 part numbers for GE. Trained inspectors for Pratt & Whitney, GE, and Rolls-Royce customer quality requirements.

AEROSPACE ENGINEERING INTERNATIONAL, continued

**Achievements as Quality Manager**
- Pioneered sampling plan inspection process — reduced standard rework at final inspection for $80K annual savings, decentralized inspection, and introduced operator certification program with self-inspection.
- Improved annual throughput $55K by launching operator certification process to expedite in-line inspections for tip mill, airfoil peening, and root peening.
- Prevented chronic engine breakdowns and reworks by discovering root cause and fixing tip length failure issue.
- Saved $6K annually correcting coating thickness for antigall and varnish applications by establishing calibration and measurement processes using Fischer Dualscope.

**Quality Engineer** (1998-2000)
Contributed to ISO 9002 Certification (internal audits, ISO training, and procedure-writing). Created manufacturing/quality work instructions for new and mature parts. As Statistical Process Control Coordinator, gained customer approval to use expanded tolerances on applicable dimensional characteristics.

- Reduced annual scrap by $55K as Chair of Manufacturing Corrective Action Board.
- Six Sigma Green Belt — reduced annual chord width scrap by $19K and platform mismatch scrap by $16K.
- Reduced development time from 8 months to 5 months for General Electric and Rolls-Royce.

CREDIT SYSTEM SERVICES, INC., Montgomery, AL                    1997 to 1998
Leading U.S. credit card processor (Bank of America, Chase, CitiBank, and Federal Government).

**Project Analyst**
Analyzed client project requests and translated into business specifications for programming staff.
- Reduced rejection rate from 3% to 0.6% by driving improvements in quality standards and performance measures. Improved turnaround from 48 hours to 24 hours.
- Built $30MM revenue for client managing Phase I of Change-In-Terms.

SENTRY FOODS, Savannah, GA                    1993 to 1997
$500mm frozen food processor supplying Burger King, Sysco, Sam's Club, and other retail food outlets.

*Drove team efforts to deliver continuous improvement in process, cost, quality, and productivity.*

**Production Coordinator**
- Reduced annual labor cost by $41K, as Team Leader for line 5 Continuous Process Improvement Team.
- Increased third shift running rate efficiency from 68% to 86%.
- Improved weekly product yields from loss of 1200 #s to gain of 120 #s.
- Improved on time startup efficiency from 43% to 81%.
- Captured annual cost savings of $18K implementing SPC for line 5 packaging equipment.

COCA-COLA FOODS, Jacksonville, FL                    1989 to 1993

*Reduced annual cost by $168K optimizing solids collection in 4 aseptic bulk tank preparation seasons.*

**Production Supervisor**
- Directed team of 63 monitoring storage of over $19MM aseptic orange juice, earning recognition for maintaining product integrity for 18 months.
- Benchmarked 8-hour shift production record for 4 non-fitment fillers.
- Increased plastic bottle line running rate efficiency from 64% to 93%.
- Achieved zero lost workday accident record for 3 years.
- Co-wrote manuals for startup procedures/standard operating procedures and equipment monitoring check lists.

## Education

M.B.A., Business Administration, Columbus State University, Columbus, GA

B.S., Animal Science, Virginia Polytechnic Institute, Blacksburg, VA

# CHRISTY R. REYES

3820 Pond Ridge Roade
Wilson, North Carolina 27893

creyes@aol.com

(919) 588-0776 [H]
(262) 872-0837 [C]

## VICE PRESIDENT / SENIOR MANAGER
### STRATEGIC PLANNING – CHANGE MANAGEMENT – BUSINESS DEVELOPMENT

*Vice President level leadership with 24 years of experience. Business development and operational executive focused on developing highly effective strategies and systems that streamline operations, increase revenue, and maximize productivity. Creative, decisive and action oriented leader. Sustained performances with record results through numerous operational areas.*

### CORE COMPETENCY AREAS

| | | |
|---|---|---|
| Executive Level Business Development | Process Reengineering | Trainer of High-Performance Teams |
| Business Process Design / Planning | Productivity Increases / Operational Efficiency | Technical Product Development |
| Organizational Structuring | Restructuring / Change Management | Global Operations Management |
| Performance Optimization / Goal Setting | Organizational Turnarounds | Assertive / Independent / Business leader |
| Budget Planning / Portfolio Analysis | Analytical and Innovative Problem Solving | Calculated Risk Taker / Innovative Thinker |
| Competitive Benchmarking Activities | Internal & External Communications Expert | Persuasive Presentation Techniques |

### PROFESSIONAL PROFILE

**24 Years Experience as a Corporate Executive and Operational Leader**
- Executive leader focused on strategic, financial and operational excellence. Expertise in the areas of operational planning, organizational structuring, and performance optimization. Twenty-four years of experience as a senior level management team member who can sustain revenue and reach margin attainment goals, ensuring the highest standards of quality and customer service.
- Key director and promoter of organizational policy design, structure, goals, and objectives set by the CEO and Board of Directors. Draws on a broad range of industry experience in the areas of technical product development and global technology management.
- Proven ability to drive overall results and revitalize performance while achieving budgetary requirements during active reengineering and change management initiatives. Innovative and creative problem solver, who methodically develops systems and plans to reorganize, streamline, and integrate productivity strategies into organizations.
- Visionary leader who champions short-term/long-range plans and budgets based on comprehensive corporate and expansion objectives. Spearheads the development, communication, and implementation of effective growth strategies and the development of more efficient processes and financial controls.

**Highly Respected Director of Corporate Policy Design & Organizational Realignment**
- Astute knowledge of the design, development, and implementation of appropriate procedures and controls that promote effective communication and information flow throughout the organization.
- Establishes all operating policies consistent with the CEO's overall vision for growth and expansion. Ensures that all activities are in compliance with local, state, and federal regulations and laws governing business operations.
- Adept in the use of instruments and metrics to systematically track and evaluate operational changes and report these results to senior management. Provides concise reports on the operating condition and company profitability in a timely and accurate manner.
- Collaborates with management teams on the development of operational infrastructure systems, processes, and teams that are designed to support rapid growth projections.
- Proven leader across a variety of global, corporate, engineering, administrative, and supply chain functions. Exceptional leadership in: issue identification, job realignment/competencies improvements, technology implementation, goal setting, and integration of sustainable business improvements. A proven change agent and internal consultant to C-Level leaders and staff.

**Senior People Manager and Developer of Effective Management Teams**
- Expertise in building and leading cross-functional teams to transition companies from under-performing entities to streamlined, profitable organizations, maximizing performance and operational effectiveness. Enjoys international travel and large group training.
- Oversee management teams and directors who coordinate department activities, drive programs, and develop the structure in which employees can function effectively and serve as a unified team to reach goals.

# CHRISTY R. REYES

## PROFESSIONAL EXPERIENCE

**DOVER CONSULTING, INC.**, Black Creek, NC
**President (2008 – Present)**
Proof of Performance & Responsibilities Highlights:

» *Provider of project and process management, and strategic planning for profit and non-profit organizations.*

- Direct and lead growth for this upstart consulting firm. Design and developed sales plans, marketing messages and materials, corporate and new market expansion strategies.
- Coach and mentor Executive Directors through the development and successful implementation of strategies to eliminate financial debt issues that threaten client operations, profitability, and corporate stability.
- Conduct time, program, and business management training for Executive and C-Level leadership, as well as for their staff and volunteer work force. Presented seminars and training to Non-Profit organizations focused on the elimination of leader work overload and substantial increase in staff productivity and organizational effectiveness.
- Consulting serves include personal training, performance recommendations, C-Level reporting, activity planning, time and employee management functions, information development for the Board of Directors, establishing vendor performance criteria, hiring strategies, and organizational growth strategies.

**BUELL MOTORCYCLE COMPANY**, East Troy, WI
**Senior Account Executive (2006 – 2007)**
Proof of Performance & Responsibilities Highlights:

» *Focused on remedying root cause problems to ensure solutions were effectively integrated into larger systems without causing adverse results. Provide holistic solutions that lead to established sustainable results.*
» *Overachieved budgetary compliance target allowing company to reduce overall spending by $25 million while increasing the number of quality and technology projects undertaken within the first year.*
» *Introduced new process for product technology planning with a 38% improvement in internal product planning acceptance rates. This improvement rate is defined as:*
  » *Number of research projects included in new product plans after process change*
  » *2005 – 2006, department documented a 37% increase after eliminating factors affecting implementation rate*
» *Championed global performance tracking and reporting processes with 100% implementation and significant improvements in technology delivery to various engineering organizations.*
» *Created, sponsored, and implemented senior officer and senior executive technology immersion event leading to increased efforts within the company to implement customer-focused technologies. Examples of Buell products changed as a result of information learned in the event –Buell's new use of YouTube for videos showing Buell products, Buell's corporate website content.*

- **Managed the corporate $585+ advanced technology budget** for global operations. Accomplished this by collaborating with executive and research teams to create annual work plans for the budget and negotiating funding levels so that the budget target was met without being exceeded, and the monitoring/tracking of team performance. Won the support of the VP, Executive Director, and staff to restructure the budgeting process real while developing budget parameters for the following year.
- **Revamped technology development processes**, tools, and management activities within the assessment process and implementation performance metrics revision.
- Key performance and operational redesign areas included:
  » *Championing the team revision of the IT database*
  » *Leading the Financial Department in the improvement of their research and development budget*
  » *Collaborated with California and Canadian based teams to ensure budgets were drafted and implemented*
  » *Created VP and executive Director presentation packages on budgets for review by the CEO and staff*
  » *Lead department staff to incorporate milestones reporting and progress review strategies*
  » *Developed a report system that transparently reported upcoming budget issues and proposed solutions*
- **Created a fully integrated global organization supporting engineering operations** associated with advanced technology development. Made proposal to allow overseas teams to take increased ownership on the management of their budgets and to provide them with voting rights for any removal of funds from their regions prior to actions being taken. Increased communication effectiveness between researchers and Buell product engineers.

CONTINUED »»

# CHRISTY R. REYES

## PROFESSIONAL EXPERIENCE

- **Lead department reorganization driving technology project delivery time and product implementation improvements**. These included work performance enhancements, increasing overall morale, understanding the "big picture" on a micro-employee level. This was successfully accomplished by reviewing department deliverables, interviewing employees to determine department history, determining value-add and non-value add man-hours, identification of key customer groups and expectations, ensuring staff buy-in to the corporate vision for growth and change, creative and reformative evaluation of employee job skills, weekly one-on-one review sessions, and the making of recommendations on restructuring strategies based on these findings.
- **Managed global staff information exchange in the U.S., Europe, and Asia-Pacific**. Provided critical input to supplier technology capability assessments: held monthly email reports to upper management, engineers, and scientists to keep them informed of major decisions; held bi-weekly meetings with employees in non-US regions to review work assignments and progress reports; communicated with executives in other regions to interview and hire employees to be matrixed into the department; created a formal organizational chart with vision and mission statements that were approved by all global executives showing how teams synergistically implemented cross-functional responsibilities.
- **Provided input to supplier technology capability assessments and served as speaker at conferences** on future technology trends within the global automotive industry. Made presentations to Buell's California research team, speaking to company expectations on new ideas that the team could bring to the table given their exposure to Silicon Valley and the entertainment industry. Made presentations to China, South Korea, and Australia; made presentations to NCSU about the overall changes in the future automotive industry in the areas of hybrids, electronics, manufacturing, materials, and safety.

**BUELL MOTORCYCLE COMPANY, East Troy, WI**
**Director of Vehicle Performance and Engineering Fleet (2003 – 2004)**
Proof of Performance & Responsibilities Highlights:

> » *Reduced budgetary expenses by 28% while improving asset delivery performance to 100%*
> » *Successfully restructured the organization enabling cost reduction through the elimination of expenses associated with 85 contract resources.*
> » *Championed the development of a new cost reduction team and idea generation methodology, which allowed for material cost reduction at the fully integrated product levels.*
> » *Familiar with asset management methods (PPAP, TQM, Six-SIGMA) for measuring operational and design capabilities.*

- Led activities bringing department into budgetary compliance while improving corporate management performance of mobile engineering assets. Familiarization with fully integrated product testing procedures.
- Directed a 90-person department and 7000+ unit mobile assets in support of product testing and competitive benchmarking activities.
- Managed shipping and freight operations, increasing efficiencies, tracking, budgeting, and inventory controls.

## FORMAL EDUCATION

**UNIVERSITY OF WISCONSIN**, Madison, WI
*Master of Business Administration (MBA), 1999*

**ALVERNO COLLEGE**, Milwaukee, WI
*Bachelor of Science, Industrial Engineering, 1985*

## HONORS & AFFILIATIONS

- ► Latino Women in Engineering, National Award for Career Achievement in Technology and Business (2004)
- ► Member of the President's Council of Alverno College Women (2004 – Present)
- ► Keynote Speaker for University of Wisconsin's 1st Motorcycle Technology Conference (2006)
- ► Member of the National Association of Hispanic MBAs (2006 – Present)

# Yolanda Rodriguez

yrodriguez@emailme.com • (617) 555-2240

*"Good HR propels good business"*

---

**SENIOR HUMAN RESOURCES OPERATIONS EXECUTIVE**
Benchmarking Business Partner . . . Consultative Training, Development & Leadership Programs

---

*"Yolanda is without a doubt one of the best HR professionals I have had the opportunity to work with over the past 30 years. She is a fighter who does not give up on something she believes in that will add value to an organization."* – Vice President of Human Resources, Software Solutions

### Deep Expertise

HR/OD Best Practices
Change Management
Employee Morale & Engagement
Affirmative Action Plans
Performance Management Systems
Retention & Productivity Improvement
Workplace Investigations
Restructuring & Integration

### Certifications

Zenger-Miller Leadership Program
DDI Management
TQM

**Influential change agent and unifier** crafting robust consultative HR models that stimulate profitable business partnerships; develop talent and career paths; leverage diversity; and elevate HR department credibility and value.

Standout success protecting companies from legal exposure, banking on multi-faceted approach to workplace investigations with comprehensive resolution and follow through.

Diverse industry experience – high technology, health care, software, and services – within smaller business and global corporate arenas.

**Team mentor and champion**, energized by helping teams move and excel through change. Migrated two HR generalists to senior leadership roles supporting 500-person account.

### *Recent Career Highlights*

- Cut penalty payouts $350,000 to client company (BCBSVA) within 6 months of program restructure improving production and service quality levels of highly resistant 600+ staff. Eliminated nearly all financial penalties within a year.

- Acquisition Integration Leader – Retained 100% of uniquely skilled employee base for client company transitioning 200 employees through change from private to publicly traded company. Integrated all HR functions within 4 months with no disruption to operations.

---

**HUMAN RESOURCES MANAGEMENT EXPERIENCE**
**Encouraging a culture of accountability, engagement, and ownership across operations.**

---

YALE SYSTEMS, Franklin, VA                                                                 2003 to Present
$2.3 billion global Fortune 1000 firm delivering industry-specific technology-based business solutions.

**HR Senior Manager** (2005-present)
Propel improvements in team performance and sustain high-quality HR service levels to 1700+ Yale associates. Concurrent sole HR Consultant for 7 Yale accounts with diverse HR imperatives, including CVS, Owens & Minor, and a major medical center.

Drove comprehensive change management initiatives for BCBSVA and HTTS (IT services, HelpDesk, application development, technical project management, and business process operations involving claims processing and quality). Critical contributions include:

BCBSVA   • Designed and launched Q&A interactive website to educate employees on new Incentive
                 Compensation Plan.
               • Inspired high performance culture implementing Gung Ho, Lean and Kaisen principles.

HTTS       • Retained 95% of top performers following transition of HR services to a Yale competitor. HPHC
                 rescinded request for early termination of Perot contract.
               • Innovated communications campaign – Q&A website, weekly CEO e-mail updates, monthly all
                 hands meetings, change management classes, stress-less classes, retention bonus program.

---

**YALE SYSTEMS,** continued

**HR Manager** (2003-2005)
Supported 1300 associates serving 4 key health care industry accounts. Directed 5 HR Generalists and 3 Training Specialists.

SOFTWARE SOLUTIONS, INC., Greenwich, VT                    1998 to 2003
Global provider of B2B software products to Fortune 500 companies.

**HR Manager**
Strategic business partner, creating business solutions with executives, managers, and employees around mergers and acquisitions, consolidations, restructures, and business plans.

☐ Partnered with CEOs of 4 start-up subsidiaries to align HR initiatives with company's brand. Drove advances in key areas: management and team development; executive and technical recruitment; employee relations; compensation and benefits.

☐ HR Specialist for merger, integration and consolidation of new company. As site Project Manager, innovated corporate vision, mission, goals, and values, collaborating with top management and employee-based team.

STANFORD MEDICAL ASSOCIATES, Westport, VT                    1996 to 1998

**HR Generalist**
Led HR function for two full scale medical centers with unique business challenges and distinct leadership teams. Resolved complex performance issues through launch of improvement plans, progressive discipline, mutual separation agreements, management coaching, and employee counseling. Partnered with management to design Staff Morale Improvement Initiative that included staff surveys, open forums, and employee self-directed work teams.

RAYTHEON COMPANY                    1984 to 1996

**Manager - Training, Employee Relations**
**Manager - Employee Relations, Affirmative Action, Community Relations**
**Specialist - Technical/Non-Technical Employment, Affirmative Action**

One of three people recruited every two years for specialized internal HR program, with accountability for employment, compensation, benefits, training, affirmative action, and employee relations at corporate offices, research and development labs, and manufacturing facilities.

☐ Skilled presenter and program facilitator on diverse HR issues – performance management, union avoidance, sexual harassment, confidentiality, Family Medical Leave and Americans with Disabilities Acts.

☐ Despite tight time frames and challenging DOD requirements, consistently earned letters of compliance managing several government on-site reviews.

---

## EDUCATION

**HR Strategic Management Program**, Harvard Business School
Partnered with CEOs and HR executives in week-long program.

**B.A., Psychology/Human Resources**, Boston College, Chestnut Hill, MA

# MARY D. SHARPER

**College Address:**
215 Robin Lane, Apt. 55
State College, PA 16801

724-755-4132
msharp6134@psu.edu

**Permanent Address:**
2530 Foxfire Drive
Harrisville, PA 16038

## EVENT PLANNING · HOSPITALITY MANAGEMENT

High-energy, highly organized achiever with solid work ethic. Thrive in challenging, multi-project and deadline-driven situations. Able to work independently and attend to myriad details without losing sight of big picture. Solid interpersonal as well as oral and written communication skills. Readily establish rapport with individuals at all professional levels and from diverse backgrounds. Computer skills include Microsoft Word, Excel, PowerPoint, and Internet communication and research. Conversant in Spanish.

## EDUCATION

**Bachelor of Science**, anticipated May 2008, Pennsylvania State University – University Park, PA
**Hotel, Restaurant and Institutional Management** · Dean's List every semester · GPA 3.84

- ✓ Meetings and Events Planning I, II
- ✓ Hospitality Management I, II
- ✓ Hospitality Managerial Accounting
- ✓ Food Prep and Presentation
- ✓ Adv. Food Production & Service Management
- ✓ Organizational Behavioral Hospitality Management
- ✓ Hospitality Finance
- ✓ Wine Appreciation

Kappa Omicron Nu (Health and Human Development Honors Society), Member

Hospitality Committee Member for THON (fundraising marathon benefiting The Four Diamonds Fund, Conquering Pediatric Cancer, at the Penn State Children's Hospital in Hershey, PA) – served on 20-member subcommittee preparing and serving food for 700+ dancers and hundreds of volunteers and supporters.

## CERTIFICATION/PROFESSIONAL ASSOCIATION

ServSafe Certification · Club Managers Association of America, Penn State Student Chapter

## INTERNSHIPS

**CATERING/EVENT INTERN, Parkway Country Club** – Harrisville, PA        *Winter Break 2007 – 2008*
- Key member of team to work in banquet facility with capacity for 400 people.

**CATERING/EVENT INTERN, Pine Tree Country Club** – Warren, OH        *May 2007 – August 2007*
- Participated in client meetings; suggested meal/bar options that increased revenue. Took initiative to suggest set-up alternatives that resulted in better efficiency and more attractive event experience for up to 225 guests.
- Used critical thinking abilities to troubleshoot problems and concerns as they arose. Dialoged with banquet servers to improve morale and ensure efficient event production.

## WORK EXPERIENCE

**BANQUET SERVER, Ocean City Convention Center** – Ocean City, MD        *May 2006 – August 2006*
- Recognized by management for dependability. Prepared for and served at numerous banquets and events with 200 to 2,000 attendees. Gained experience in effective food preparation, organizational skills and time management.

**SERVER, Seacoast Specialties** – Ocean City, MD        *May 2006 – August 2006*
- Courteously and efficiently served food and beverages to clientele in main restaurant as well as for private functions and parties. Received praise from customers for being patient and personable.
- Recognized by manager for delivering world-class customer service. Entrusted to monitor and oversee private events.

**CREW LEADER, Breaker's Real Ice Cream** – Harrisville, PA        *February 2004 – January 2006*
- Promoted to crew leader after two months. In absence of manager or assistant manager, supervised crew members, resolved customer issues, monitored product availability and managed close-out procedures.
- Originated promotional ideas/slogans for marquee that boosted revenue and increased repeat clientele.
- Assisted in training new associates as well as manager-trainees in efficient service and operational strategies.

## PERSONAL STRENGTHS

*Descriptive terms of personal strengths in the workplace based on Professional Behavioral Profiling*

. . . Optimistic ~ Innovative ~ Tenacious ~ Negotiates conflicts ~ Motivates others toward goals

# MELANIE SIMMONS

2000 Lake Drive
West Farmington, Ohio 44491

Home: 330-481-7263
melsims@yahoo.com

## EDUCATOR — GUIDANCE COUNSELOR — K–12
## ELEMENTARY AND SECONDARY ADMINISTRATOR

*Melanie Simmons unquestionably stands in the very top echelon [of 40 high school counselors with whom I have interacted]. She is well organized, proactive in her approach to problems, and demonstrates a true compassion for students.*

*[Melanie] has developed excellent relationships with home school administrators and counselors. Her judgment is sound and her perspective on issues is never tainted with bias. She is current with educational research but is mindful of common sense approach to problems.*

*Melanie has excellent potential to work in the administrative field. She navigates the fine line that exists between her role as a counselor and the perspectives of administrators.*

*The basis for effective leadership is the ability to make informed decisions and to communicate with the parties concerned. Melanie does this routinely. She sees the big picture and her demeanor is always professional.*

*—Len Collins*
*Academic Supervisor*
*Warren Career &*
*Technical Center*

✓ Highly regarded educator and leader committed to preparing students, teachers, and members of the school community to learn, live, and succeed in a pluralistic society through understanding and appreciating the uniqueness of individuals.

✓ Utilize teaching skills to promote a lifelong love of learning in children, adolescents, and young adults. Create an energizing educational experience that motivates students to achieve physical, academic, and personal accomplishment to the best of their ability.

✓ Provide leadership for professional and administrative staff in development, implementation, and evaluation of comprehensive educational programs. Administer programs in accordance with school board policies and administrative rules and regulations. Actively develop and maintain positive parent and community relations.

✓ Motivated to implement new ideas, troubleshoot, and take the initiative in major projects. Selected to serve on county's Crisis Intervention Team.

✓ Savvy in managing budgets.

## PROFESSIONAL EXPERIENCE

**Warren Career and Technical Center** – West Farmington, Ohio      *1997 – Present*
**SUPERVISOR** *(2007 – Present)*

* Supervise 29 staff in five main areas: College Tech Prep Programs, Business and Health Programs, Guidance Department, and Marketing Education Program. Manage budgets totaling $250K. Oversee student enrollment, recruitment, scheduling, and grade reporting.

* Direct implementation of curriculum and technology in the classrooms. Contribute to development and implementation of content standards.

* Key member of district leadership team and chairperson for community outreach and grading policy committees.

* Played key role in developing and maintaining nationally recognized "Project Lead the Way" curriculum in engineering program. Introduced "High Schools That Work" reform initiative district-wide. Presented "College Preview" transition program at regional and state conferences in 2007.

**GUIDANCE COUNSELOR** *(1997 – 2007)*

* Provided high school guidance counselor services to 1100 students in 11th and 12th grades in school that offers 38 career and technical program choices to students from 19 affiliate school districts in Trumbull County. Approximately one-third of this student population has special needs.

* As member of leadership team, spearheaded "High Schools That Work" improvement/reform model.

* Orchestrated student recruitment and retention initiatives. Coordinated tours and planned all aspects of annual "Career Days."

*Continued on next page*

*Warren Career and Technical Center, continued*

- Facilitated individual and group counseling sessions for students. Used ranking and performance data to discuss students' post-secondary educational options as well as for scheduling classes, providing career guidance, and offering remedial opportunities.

- Regularly interacted with parents, associate school counselors, and administrators. Acted as liaison between prospective and current students with their home school districts.

- Coordinated and administered state proficiency and competency analysis profile assessments. Co-chaired grading policy focus team.

- Implemented school-wide Advisor/Advisee Program that teamed groups of 10 students with an adult mentor. This regular interaction in group sessions made a positive impact on the school environment.

**Ohio School Counselor Association**                          *1999 – 2001*
**DISTRICT 2 REPRESENTATIVE**
- Organized and scheduled educational and professional growth opportunities for school counselors in 6-county area in northeastern Ohio. Provided networking opportunities and updates on proposed changes for school counselor licensure. Consistently worked within budget.

**Hartman Middle Schools** – Kinsman, Ohio                    *1995 – 1997*
**GUIDANCE COUNSELOR**
- Initiated individual and group guidance and counseling sessions at elementary and middle school levels. Produced report cards and accurately entered data into EMIS. Coordinated special education and standardized testing sessions.

**Beckett Local Schools** – Burghill, Ohio                    *1988 – 1995*
**CHORAL DIRECTOR AND ELEMENTARY VOCAL MUSIC TEACHER**

**Lebanon Local Schools** – Lebanon, Ohio                     *1984 – 1988*
**VOCAL MUSIC TEACHER**

## CERTIFICATIONS / LICENSURE

State of Ohio
Five-Year License, Elementary Principal
Permanent Professional, School Counselor K-12
Five-Year Professional, Music K-12, Drama-Theater

Commonwealth of Pennsylvania
Principal, K-12
Elementary and Secondary School Counselor

## EDUCATION / CONTINUING EDUCATION

Elementary and Secondary Administration Certification, 2004
Westminster College – New Wilmington, Pennsylvania

Master of Science, Education, 1995
Bachelor of Music, 1983
Youngstown State University – Youngstown, Ohio

# Rebecca Small

1220 SMITH STREET, CLIFTON PARK, NY 12065 • C: 518-339-4548 • REBECCA@SMALL.NET

## AWARD WINNING CREATIVE DIRECTOR

*Crystallizing the organization's vision through brand-on, strategy-on, and cost-conscious compelling creative electronic, interactive media, and print campaigns.*

- 12 years' experience managing creative teams to deliver web/print material that re-brand organizations, elevate public awareness of products and services, and recruit top talent for the organization.

- Proven success building value-added support service models from scratch that are client-centric, reliable, cost efficient, and revenue driven.

- Expertise translating client vision into marketing collateral that are content rich, visually appealing, functional, and easy to navigate.

### CORE COMPETENCIES

| | | |
|---|---|---|
| • Branding and Identity Campaigns | • Web Content Development | • Cross-Functional Management |
| • Project Planning and Pricing | • Website Design and Navigation | • Staff Recruitment |
| • Resource Allocation | • Print Content Development | • Staff Development/Mentoring |
| • Production Scheduling | • Art/Interactive Design Direction | • Account Management |
| • Workflow Management/Analysis | • Web and Print Content Editing | • Client Servicing |
| • Market Research/Focus Groups | • Interactive Media Production | • Client Briefs and Contracts |
| • Budgeting and Forecasting | • Advertising/Public Relations | • Speechwriting/Book Indexing |

### PROFESSIONAL EXPERIENCE

STATE UNIVERSITY OF NEW YORK AT ALBANY, ALBANY, NY      **1999 to Present**

**Associate Director** *(2001 to Present)* - Manage strategic direction of web and print branding and identity campaigns for eight university campuses representing 963 degree programs. Drive content development and project execution for 100 single and multi-phase and multi-page projects annually. Oversee cross-functional team of ten information architects, content specialists, interactive art directors, designers, and technologist and web application developers/programmers. Budget: $2M; Creative Staff Hours: 15,000

*Process Improvements and Revenue Gains*

- Accelerated creative services group revenues from zero to over 2 million dollars annually by transforming department from a base funded unit to a fee-for-services model.

- Achieved goal of 70% billable hour rate within first year following transition, captured new clients, and established department as a competitively priced and reliable service by meticulously monitoring billable hours and determining project cycle time estimates that closely matched real time production results.

- Consistently delivered projects on-time and on-budget and improved project forecasting capabilities exponentially by introducing the group's inaugural workflow management systems to monitor billable hours, track project milestones, and establish project schedules and budgets.

- Created vision for and led university's first cross-department, cross-functional web standards group to implement "must practices" and "best practices", standardize university branding efforts across campuses and departments, and build project management efficiencies. Achieved status as decision making body with support from senior administrative members just one year after group was formed.

*Notable Projects*

- **10 Great Things About SUNYA** (www.greatsunya.edu) - Conceived concept for, wrote copy, and marshaled team resources to develop interactive content for one of the most successful marketing campaigns in the university's history that included traditional print and electronic messaging strategies (website, brochure, billboards). Measurable results included 370,000 pages viewed since campaign launched two years ago, an 18% increase in applications between 2006 and 2007, and admission of a 2007 freshman class with record setting entrance scores and the highest high school averages noted to date.

1

# Rebecca Small

C: 518-339-4548 • REBECCA@SMALL.NET

*Notable Projects (continued)*

- **School of Health, Physical Education, and Recreation** (http://www.hper.sunya.edu) - Elevated awareness of school's academic diversity, streamlined site navigations, and improved functionality by redesigning site and incorporating more on-brand images and student profiles.

- **James School of Music** (http://www.music.sunya.edu) - Shaped communication of school's core brand and increased pages viewed from 2004 to 2006 from 27,000 to 32,000 by redesigning site to leverage leading-edge technologies including an online audio player with faculty and student performances and a flash tour of the school's facilities. Built community and interest by publishing a timeline of the school's history, profiles of the distinguished faculty, and access to an online music store.

- **School of Nursing** (http://www.nursing.sunya.edu) - Enhanced school's reputation as one of the top nursing schools in the country and raised awareness of curriculum and career paths by reengineering site to include comprehensive information about degrees and majors and highlighting success stories from alumni.

- **YouTube Video Series** (www.youtube.com/sunya.edu) - Pioneered a series of *YouTube* videos to increase university awareness among perspective students online; garnered 1,500+ channel views in just three months and drew attention from the news media and other universities.

*Recent Industry Awards*

- 2007 Web Award - competed against 8,000 entrees; winning status as Best School Website.

- 2006 Web Awards official honoree for National Science Olympiad website

- 2006 W3 Gold Award in Science category winner for University Life Sciences website and silver award in science category for National Science Olympiad web site.

- 2005 multiple gold, silver, and bronze Education Pinnacle Awards for four websites and two print brochures.

***Manager of Marketing Publications*** *(1999 to 2001)* - Selected to blend together a traditional print communications team with a newly created web development team. Tasked with developing a formalized and measurable process for delivery schedules and client agreements within a culture with previous limited accountability in these areas.

- Created concept for, wrote, designed, and launched *College Now* brochure to promote the importance of higher education to middle school children and their parents. Brochure received national acclaim and continues to be republished annually.

- Developed vision for a school community website that authentically captured historic campus events and acts as a model for communicating information in times of crisis.

- Hand picked by President of the University to write several of his talking points and speeches, create PowerPoint presentations, and oversee event logistics.

HARROW & COMPANY ADVERTISING, ALBANY, NY                                    **1996 to 1999**

***Copywriter*** *(1998 to 1999)* charged with writing print ads, TV/radio commercials, direct mail pieces, brochures, annual reports, and books. First copywriter in agency to create content for the web.

- Recognized with Addy for best print ad from the New York State Ad Club and silver award for Excellence in Marketing from the University Continuing Education Association (UCEA).

***Public Relations Specialist*** *(1996 to 1998)* - Pitched stories to local news media and national trade publications and provided media training to clients.

---

## EDUCATION

---

Bachelor of Arts, Journalism and History, State University of New York at Buffalo, 1992

2

# LEE SMITH

29 Terrace Scotts Road
Sterling, VA 20165

(703) 212-1359
leesmith@aol.com

*Talented young professional with skills and training in:*
## RESEARCH AND PROGRAM MANAGEMENT

**Inquisitive, resourceful, quick-learner** with strong desire and aptitude for a career within the field of research and development. Regarded by peers and mentors as an overachiever who is **committed to excellence in this field**, as demonstrated by **outstanding academic achievement**. Demonstrate thorough and detailed research hypothesis forming capabilities, as well as a capacity for accurately testing and analyzing resulting data for presentation of written findings. Experienced in project coordination and logistics support for research, evaluation, training projects. *Experience and academic preparation include:*

- Methods of Psychology
- Contemporary Economics
- Publicity Campaign Development

- Psychology Tests/Measurements
- Program Evaluation/Assessment
- Training Program Development

- Advanced Statistics
- Financial Data Analysis
- Microsoft Office Suite

## EDUCATION

**Bachelor of Arts in Psychology**
Shepherd University, Shepherdstown, WV ~ 5/2006

## RELEVANT EXPERIENCE & EMPLOYMENT

**Program Director** ~ McLean Air Force Base Community Center, McLean VA ~ 9/2006 to present
**Teacher** ~ Montessori Child Development Center, Kearneysville WV ~ 1/2006 to 5/2006
**Audio/Visual Media Tech** ~ Marymount Audio/Visual Media Center, Marymount VA ~ 1/2006 to 5/2006
**Mentor/Tutor** ~ Sterling Youth Center, Sterling VA ~ 8/2004 to 5/2005
**Homeland Security Guard** ~ Langley Air Force Base, Langley VA ~ 6/2004 to 8/2004

- *Athletics Research Project Management:* Tirelessly worked to prove hypothesis about *"Athletes and Ankle and Knee Injuries"* at Shepherd University. Spent almost a full year gathering data, developing surveys, administering them to athletes and consolidating data into SPSS, resulting in a project conclusion with clearly defined results. Project garnered rave reviews, and was awarded an outstanding grade due to emphasis on research collection, collaboration with students and faculty, and project execution.

- *Program Evaluation & Assessment:* Evaluated long-range community programs based on available resources and the needs of the military community, and developed both on and off base community programs.

- *Mentoring & Tutoring:* Assisted students with academic achievement and served as a positive role model by creating diverse and engaging post tutor session programming, easing the struggles of young adulthood and aiding students with employability, life and social skills.

- *Reporting and Documentation:* Established and safeguarded an accurate log of personnel incidents and events at Norfolk Naval Base. Partnered with security guard teams to safeguard the base ground.

- *Cost Savings:* Generated alternate solutions to raise and save money for programs such as "Breakfast with Santa" and "Colossal Cookie Bake-Off", reducing operating expenses by 88%, and offering more corporate exposure to military personnel via newly developed sponsorships and advertising opportunities.

- *Budget Proposal & Finance Analysis:* Prepared multi-departmental annual operating budget and quarterly revisions and submitted for approval to Community Center Director. Compiled, consolidated and analyzed program and financial data, enabling faster and more efficient data retrieval.

- *Program Management:* Acted as Advisor for and administrator of The Congressional Award (the U.S. Congress' Award for young Americans) at Langley Air Force Base. Outlined volunteer requirements for military personnel, organized event logistics, and delivered participant awards.

## MEMBERSHIPS & VOLUNTEER EXPERIENCE

American Psychology Association ~ Young Filipino Professionals of Hampton Road

# LAURA SOLON, PMP

1222 NE Pine St. · Pullman, CA 93005 · (555) 555-5555 · LauraSolon@email.com

*Good software changes business and changes to meet business needs.*

## SUMMARY OF QUALIFICATIONS

Award-winning IT leader and entrepreneur with record of leading development of industry-changing software. Led 3 Silicon Valley start-ups to multi-million-dollar sales. Sought-after seminar presenter with expertise in design patterns, emergent design, and programming for Agile software development. Outstanding staff development, business facilitation, and communication skills. Analytical, intuitive, and articulate.

## CORE COMPETENCIES

| | | |
|---|---|---|
| Business Development | Project Leadership | Software Innovation |
| Investor & Partner Relations | Policy & Procedure Development | System Optimization |
| Change Management | Public Speaking | Quality Assurance |

## PROFESSIONAL EXPERIENCE

**MCBEAN MANAGEMENT SYSTEMS**, Sunnyvale, CA
*Vice President, Customer Satisfaction & Quality Assurance* (2005 – Present)
*Development Manager* (2002 – 2005)
*Directed team of 63 to provide excellent customer support for state-of-the-art document management software licensed to more than 50% of Fortune 100 companies. Developed and coached team consisting of call center, lab, shipping, and technical staff. Continuously identified opportunities for enhanced profitability.*

- Led segment of company that ***produced 56% of total revenue*** for start up company.
- Achieved 81% gross margin in maintenance revenues (approximately $45 million) by driving innovation of new applications and decreasing time-to-market.
- ***Reduced cost-per-incident 15%*** by implementing process improvements following in-depth time studies.
- Enhanced self-service capabilities offered on Support Direct website; added feature to view customer incidents and opening incidents on website
- ***Increased sales by $1 million/quarter*** in extremely sluggish market; improved services support via hot incidents call, customer outreach program, and major accounts initiative.
- Managed quality assurance staff of 25 to provide enhanced certification testing for 4 new products.
- Guided new initiatives, including: population of test repository and automation of tests using Mercury tools, developing teams dedicated to integration and performance testing, establishing maintenance-only QA cycles to expedite delivery of fixes to customers in service packs, and publishing of test plans before and weekly results during test cycle.
- Directed 25 + resources in India, resulting in *cost savings of 9.4% within first year* and further savings of 2.3% in second year via weekly resource development Web conferences.

**INTELLISPACE**, Sunnyvale, CA
*Chief Information Officer* (1997 – 2001)
*Planned, created, and staffed IT Departments for this start-up company. Designed product line and directed development to facilitate rapid expansion into education software market. Pitched business plans and technical capabilities to potential investors to secure $60 million in funding.*

- Developed architectural strategy and modular development plan to *accelerate time-to-market by 15%.*
- Defined requirements and managed design and delivery of Web-based Operations Support System for order management, *leapfrogging competition by 2 months*.
- Launched first-to-market virtual lab product, Xenos, *driving $6 million in sales in year 2 of business*.

*(Continued)*

**BRANDLE CORPORATION**, Cupertino, CA
***Director, Research & Development*** (1994 – 1997)
***Analyst, Research & Development*** (1990 – 1993)
*Directed design, delivery, and support of new releases and new products with sales of $90 million. Oversaw multiple teams in delivery of new product to monitor Goplex environments using proprietary Brandle infrastructure in first commercial use; earned Management Excellence Award as result. Formed division that delivered 80% of maintenance revenue with 45 analysts and 2 managers.*

- Served as Systems Manager for Brandle-wide support of 2 IBM products: Parallel Processing hardware/software and Service Level Reporter.
- As Product Owner, directed launch of new flagship product (Omega Sun) that ***contributed $80 million to company revenue***; recognized with Management Excellence Award for performance.
- Managed 10-member offshore team in Mexico charged with product support.
- Delivered enhanced middleware acquisitions to new billion-dollar market; products provided secure data transmission via encryption on various diverse platforms.
- ***Spearheaded 9 major releases*** of Historical Performance Monitors for Brandle's mainframe products and managed transition of all real-time MVS Product Development to White Plains office.
- Created Project Office to ***support 200+ projects and 380 people***; implemented Phase Gate process to ensure quality checkpoints were completed for each project in every development phase.

## EDUCATION

**WILLIAM BRANDT COLLEGE**, New London, CT
*Bachelor of Science:* Computer Engineering
*Minor:* Communication

## INDUSTRY CERTIFICATION

Project Management Professional, Project Management Institute

## TECHNICAL EXPERTISE

| | |
|---|---|
| *Languages:* | C#, C++, J#, Visual Basic.Net, PHP, and Java |
| *Operating Systems:* | Windows, Linux, and UNIX |
| *Databases:* | SQL Server, MySQL, Oracle, Informix, Sybase DB/CT, and DB2 |
| *Tools:* | Asp.Net, TDD, SOA, .Net 2.0, FIT, NUnit, CruiseControl.net, NCover, MSBuild |
| *Methodologies:* | Test Driven Development, Lean Software Development, Agile Software Development, Scrum, Good Design, Emergent Design, Design Patterns, Custom Code Generation, and Monte Carlo Modeling |

# JOHN TAYLOR SPAIN

jtspain01@yahoo.com

4198 El Dorado Parkway
McKinney, TX 75071

(972) 578-6641

## RESEARCH METHODOLOGY

Detail-oriented, experienced **Research Methodology Professional;** adept at forming hypotheses, conducting research, and drawing valid conclusions. Known for doing things in the most effective way possible, implementing technology to drive efficiency when feasible, and going the "extra mile" on projects, as needed.

Experience working on complex research projects and presenting at regional conferences. Superior interpersonal and rapport-building skills. Consistently able to get information from people when others cannot. Proven history of coaching others on best-in-class research practices. Strong follow-up skills. Fluent in Spanish.

**Computer Proficiencies:** Word, Excel, PowerPoint, Adobe Acrobat, SPSS, SAS, and Survey Pro

### Key Strengths:

- Analytical, Dedicated, and Collaborative Team Player with Stellar Work Ethic
- Culturally Sensitive and Able to Work Well with Diverse Groups of People
- Excellent Communication, Presentation, and Follow-Up Skills
- Sense of Urgency—Always Meet Deadlines

### Research Expertise:

- Conducting Quantitative and Qualitative Data Analysis
- Analyzing, Collecting, and Interpreting Statistical Data: Multiple Regression, Logistical Regression, and Path Analysis
- Writing and Executing SAS Programs
- Developing Research Methodologies, Surveys, and Research Questions / Questionnaires
- Managing Interviews and Legal Research
- Maintaining and Monitoring Research Methodologies for Quality Assurance, Reliability and Validity
- Summarizing, Organizing, and Interpreting Data from Multiple Sources
- Identifying Trends Through Data Analysis
- Providing Secondary Analysis for Corporate Documentation
- Writing Reports and Presenting Research Findings

## NOTABLE ACCOMPLISHMENTS:

- **Saved time and money** by innovating and automating a process to receive data from survey respondents via email; designed study using Adobe Acrobat so that when data was received, it was directly input into an Excel spreadsheet; current employer has since rolled out use of technology to other departments.

- **Increased survey response rate by 5%** in survey conducted with current employer; did this by following-up with individuals who did not complete survey and persuading them to complete it.

- **Played a key role in conducting and preparing a complex government research report;** current employer expects report to be published in May of 2008.

---

**PROFESSIONAL EXPERIENCE:**

US Department of Health and Human Services, McKinney, TX      2006 to Present

**PROGRAM ANALYST**

Conduct quantitative and qualitative analyses of federal healthcare data using SAS software. Provide briefings and presentations of analytical findings to senior management.

- Traveled across the U.S. conducting interviews for complex research study; one of four on team.
- Consistently achieved above-average performance ratings of "fully successful" and "exceptional" in all areas—the two highest ratings in four-point rating system.

Branson University, Dallas, TX      2003 to 2006

**TEACHING FELLOW / GRADUATE ASSISTANT**

Designed and taught four freshman-, junior-, and senior-level sociological courses that included the study of social research methods.

- Empowered students to perform better on tests by creating a Web site that provided students with access to notes of everything covered in class, including PowerPoint presentations.

A&M University, College Station, TX      2000 to 2002

**TEACHING ASSISTANT**

Evaluated student exams for evidence of comprehension. Maintained class Internet site. Collaborated with and assisted faculty on research studies, enabling projects to be completed ahead of schedule. Taught sociological courses as needed to provide faculty with additional time to conduct research.

Grove Property Tax Company, Pasadena, TX      1995 to 1999

**TAX CLERK**

Developed a database that enabled management to trend property tax assessments for multiple clients. This improved ability to develop reports more easily, saved time, enabled better decisions, more accurate tax assessments, and increased ability to collect more money.

**EDUCATION:**

**Bachelor of Science**, 1999
Preston Scott State University, Hunt, TX

**Master of Arts**, 2002
A&M University, College Station, TX

**Doctorate in Sociology**, 2008
Branson University, Dallas, TX

**AWARDS / HONORS:**

**WHO'S WHO AMONG STUDENTS IN COLLEGES AND UNIVERSITIES,** 1999
**OUTSTANDING SOCIOLOGY STUDENT**, 1999
A&M University, College Station, TX

**OUTSTANDING SOCIOLOGY STUDENT,** 2005
Branson University, Dallas, TX

# THOMAS L. STRONG

3799 Millenia Blvd. Orlando, FL 32838 | Phone: 407-802-4962
pkt@creatingprints.com | webres:creatingprints.com/ptk.htm

---

**Account Management | Product Marketing | Program Management—**IT Industry
*Skillfully combining sales cycle management and technical expertise to drive revenue growth*

## LEADERSHIP PROFILE

Profit-driver and technology-expert professional with more than eight years' experience exceeding sales quotas, generating increased revenue, managing highly-technical projects, and developing executive relationships. Well-rounded knowledge of the telecommunications industry with strong academic preparation: Master of Business Administration with Marketing and Management Information Systems majors; Cisco technical certifications.

### Areas of Strength

Sales Goals | Territory Sales | Marketing | Executive Presentations | Emerging Technologies | Prospecting
Consultative Sales | Negotiations | Public Speaking | New Client Acquisition | Market Assessment
Competitive Market Intelligence | Corporate Communications | Account Management | Long-term Planning
Customer Service | Networking | Product Solutions | Vendor Relations | Strategic Initiatives

~ Solid career history of sales goal deliveries ~

| Projection | Sales | Percentage |
|---|---|---|
| $240,000 | $425,000 | 177% |
| $90,000 | $106,200 | 118% |
| $102,000 | $114,000 | 112% |
| $114,000 | $123,120 | 108% |
| $185,000 | $192,816 | 104% |
| $120,000 | $121,000 | 102% |

Top performing professional with a unique ability to implement technology knowledge into sales presentations. Technical expertise: install, configure, operate, and troubleshoot medium-size routed and switched networks, including implementation and verification of connections to remote sites in a WAN.

## PROFESSIONAL EXPERIENCE & ACHIEVEMENTS

**Corporate Account Manager III**, WorldCom, Orlando, FL                    2002–Present

Sales, Marketing, and Revenue Generation:

Prospect, qualify leads, and gain new business with persuasive presentations. Lead high-powered negotiations with corporate executives; develop proposals and create enticing sales presentations that include in-depth product education and executive briefings. Combine efforts with marketing specialists to study market trends, create customized and effective marketing strategies.

→ Influenced prospective clients of fortune 1000 companies; convinced them to close on multi-million-dollar, long-term contracts by demonstrating value over the competition.
→ Managed total revenue of $5M and more than $250K per month customer revenue base.
→ Grew revenue by 10% within one year by building and strengthened relationships with existing customers.

Technology Projects:

Design and lead complex network-implementation projects. Demonstrate expertise in Wide Area Networking including IPVPN, Private IP (MPLS), Frame Relay, ATM, and Private Line; local voice and private branch exchange service including class 5 and class 3 switching technologies. Introduce emerging technologies such as VoIP, VoFR, PoE, FCoIP, hosted IP Centrex, and Managed IP PBX

→ Increased profits by selling entire suite of telecommunication products and services, leveraging partner vendors like Cisco, Nortel, Avaya, and Checkpoint.

---

**Happy About My Resume**                                                                                    **139**

**Network Solutions Consultant**, Business Solutions, Houston, TX                   2001–2002
Devised sales plans to cater to new and existing customer base and yielded higher revenue. Provided consultation on sales strategies, emerging technologies, existing line of products, and small networks to large client servers. Combined effort to work on projects that included WAN technologies, both data bandwidth and telephony solutions multiple platform networks.

→ Developed new marketing techniques that increased sales opportunities and propelled sales from $110,000 in 2000 to $425,000 in 2001.

**Network Design Consultant**, Network Media, Austin, TX                   2000–2001
Designed, installed, and maintained structured voice and data cabling projects, both Inside Plant and OSP.
Prepared bids and estimations for structured cabling projects per RFP and RFQ.

→ Collaborated and played an instrumental role in the winning bid for a $1.5M structured cabling job with the State of Texas Corrections Department.

## EDUCATION

UNIVERSITY OF TEXAS AT DALLAS, Richardson, TX
MBA, dual concentration in Management Information Systems and Marketing, 2006
Activities and Societies: National Scholars Honor Society, UTD MBA Society, AITP

TEXAS A&M UNIVERSITY, College Station, TX
Bachelor of Business Administration in Information and Operations Management, 2000

## CERTIFICATIONS

Cisco Certified Network Associate | Cisco Sales Expert

# MICHAEL SUGAR

15 West Lane　•　Des Moines, IA　•　434.555.1212　•　michaelsugar@email.com

## SENIOR SALES EXECUTIVE

Consumer & Premium Products • Business Development • U.S. & Canadian Marketplaces

*"Michael Sugar [our sales representative] does a great job…he is honorable and always available."*
- Cliff S., Buyer, ABM Home & Garden

Results-driven Sales Executive with 15+ years' experience and mastery of the consumer products industry, leveraging powerful network of contacts at specialty retailers, department stores, home shopping channels, DIY hardware channels, and mail order catalogs. Combine keen business acumen with strong grasp of client needs to design new products and expand lines. Keep pace with explosive growth of specialty retailers; serviced Bed, Bath & Beyond during expansion to 700+ stores and Linens-N-Things growth to 400+ stores. Talented forging relationships beyond front-line buyers, including relationship-building savvy with C-Level executives. Skilled pitching new business in key markets with proven track record of landing new accounts. Combine use of latest technology with face-to-face meetings in client communications; well known in industry for integrity and customer service in addition to providing tangible solutions when facing issues.

**Major Clients:** AC Moore, Bed, Bath & Beyond, The Container Store, Dr. Leonard's / Carol Wright, Hobby Lobby, HSN, JoAnn Fabrics, Linens-N-Things, Michaels Craft Stores, Miles Kimball, QVC, Rennhack Marketing Services, Ross Stores, Sears (U.S. & Canada), Solutions, Starcrest, and Wal-Mart (U.S. & Canada).

- Trends Analysis & Sales Forecasts
- Product Design & Research
- Competitive Analysis
- Merchandising & Promotions

- Team Leadership & Supervision
- Relationship Management
- Strategic Planning
- Inventory Reduction Initiatives

## PROFESSIONAL EXPERIENCE

**Director of Sales,** ALL-AGES MARKETING, LLC, DES MOINES, IA　　　　　　　2003 – Present

Key player in expansion of company's market reach and product offerings in U.S. and Canadian markets for this consumer goods (including "as-seen-on-TV" merchandise) and premium / incentive products company focused on specialty retailers, catalogers, consumers, department stores, and home shopping channels. Forged company's first-ever relationships with Bed, Bath & Beyond and Linens-N-Things retailers. Source new products, shop competition, research related product categories, and determine trends to integrate innovative and profitable ideas and products into offerings. Developed key internal initiatives, including an active newsletter and weekly sales meetings to drive team motivation and share ideas.

- Landed 75% of new business through referrals; 15% through media coverage; and 10% with incoming leads.
- Hit $11,000 per minute sales rate in first on-air feature of personally designed private-label Boundary Handbag. On target to double sales to 250,000 units – over $5M – in 2008.
- Drove $2M in single-product / single retailer sales by creating private label soldering tool for Electronics Center; pitched and won elite spot in Electronics Center's 2005 annual report.
- Landed "Today's Highlight" feature engagement on ALC Shopping Channel, generating over $500,000 in one-day sales of specialty home decorating product and relieving All-Ages of a previously overstocked item.

**New Business Sources**

Incoming Leads, 10%

Media & Outreach, 15%

Referrals, 75%

# MICHAEL SUGAR

· 434.555.1212 · michaelsugar@email.com ·

**"Michael's energy and enthusiasm for his job is unmatched."**
- Jason S., VP of Sales, House Beautiful, Inc.

**National Sales Manager**, HOUSE & HOME, INC., West Des Moines, IA        1994 – 2003

Led multi-channel distribution across U.S. and Canada for this consumer house wares company, reaching department stores, mass merchants, warehouse clubs, and specialty retailers. Serviced Bed, Bath & Beyond and Linens-N-Things retailers during explosive growth – from 40 Bed, Bath & Beyond stores to over 550 (as of 2003) and from 45 Linens-N-Things stores to over 425 in 2003. Constructed company's first-ever sales reporting system; supervised three sales and support staff along with over 40 manufacturers' representatives in both U.S. and Canada; and teamed with development to create and implement new product lines. Hired as Regional Sales Manager and promoted to National Sales Manager in 1998. Assisted company efforts in achieving ISO 2001:9000 certification for quality management systems.

- Surpassed aggressive sales goals by up to 8% annually, eight consecutive years.
- Hit 95% fulfillment rates—an all-time high—by implementing POS data monitoring on key accounts.
- Personally landed agreements with Crate & Barrel, BJ's Wholesale Club, Homeplace, Marmaxx Cos (TJ Maxx, Marshalls, Home Goods), and Home Outfitters.
- Won exclusive program and specialty department agreements with Jake & Jana, Baker Weiss, and Martha Stewart Living Omnimedia.

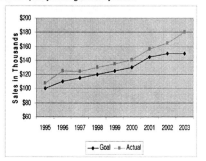

**Sales Manager,** PRICE PROMOS, INC., Des Moines, IA        1992 – 1994

Covered sales for entire U.S. region for this retail food marketing company engaged in manufacturing, importing, and marketing of promotional materials. Penetrated new markets and expanded client base 75%. Restructured operations and sales procedures to improve effectiveness while managing two sales people.

- Grew sales 25% within two years while increasing market share by expanding sales with existing customers and bringing on new accounts, including Boar's Head, D'Agostino's, and Wal-Mart.
- Streamlined client presentation process, bringing materials to 21st century with digital artwork and printing mechanics; changes resulted in 50% reduction of presentation lead-time.

## EDUCATION

**Bachelor of Arts, Psychology and French,** EMORY UNIVERSITY, Atlanta, GA

**"Thanks again for all of your help and support, it is great having vendors such as yourself who can help us out on our promotions."**
- Michael S., Category Analyst, Sears Tire

Page 2 of 2

# LAURA M. SYKES

1837 North Karlton Circle
Marshall, WI 53089

Lsykes@gmail.net
262-555-7832

## Supply Chain Management

### *International Relations . . . Purchasing . . . Logistics . . . Team Building*

High-energy, results-driven professional with international trade management background; extensive experience in directing transactions with Chinese suppliers. Extremely self-motivated with history of effectively overseeing production projects, meeting deadlines, and developing processes that promote cost-containment. Dynamic relationship influencer with ability to build consensus. Analytical and decisive planner. Proficient in Microsoft Office Suite, Microsoft Project, SAP, and various CRM, supply chain management, and Lotus software programs. Key competencies include:

- Worldwide Purchasing
- Importing & Exporting
- Supplier Management
- Global Freight Brokerage
- Expediting
- Harmonize Tariff Codes

- Distribution Management
- Inventory Control
- Staff Development
- Warehousing
- Multi-site Operations
- Quality Control

- Sourcing
- Price Negotiations
- JIT Purchasing
- Vendor Partnerships
- Product Development
- Change Management

## Career Highlights

### *HARLINGTON, INC.*

- Designed and established new international supply chain management department that increased sales for Marshall plant from $11 million to $18 million within two years by developing new major production projects and smoothly managing transition into new off-shore production operations.

- Built synergistic trade management team that has a reputation across the organization for expertise in transactions with plants in China.

- Substantially increased organizational efficiency by leading the development and implementation of trade management quality control procedures.

- Wrote change management plan for Chinese production plants, implementing strategic team structure to improve plant communications.

## Professional Experience

### *HARLINGTON, INC.*, Marshall, Wisconsin                                    2000 – Present

*Leading global consumer packaging, plastics, and beverage can producer; over $2.5 billion in annual sales.*
TRADE DESK MANAGER (2004 – Present)

Manage international supply chain management functions for cosmetics product division, which includes oversight of purchasing from six Chinese plants, developing RFQs, importing, distribution and warehousing, sales, development and implementation of production projects, pricing, order processing, customer deliveries, and inventory control. Ensure quality control, conduct cost analysis, and contribute to supply chain management planning. Supervise cross-functional team of two project managers / engineers, inside sales rep, and customer service rep. Assist Chinese plants in locating specialized raw materials using international vendor resources.

- Led development and implementation of new international production projects that contributed significantly to 63% increase in annual sales, including:
  - o Make-up compact product line, valued at $2 million.
  - o Lipstick product line, valued at $1.5 million.
  - o Mascara product line, valued at $1 million.

TRADE DESK MANAGER (Continued)
- Saved $1.5 million in production costs by turning around floundering lipstick project, infusing process and leadership to effectively resolve design and delivery issues.
- Contributed to smooth transition of production outsourcing by effectively managing customer relationships and product supply during the acquisition of plants in China.
- Introduced comprehensive supplier quality review and assessment process for products traded with Chinese facilities, helping to strengthen final product quality and production efficiency.
- Recognized as key member on several cost reduction teams; currently focusing on reducing international telephone and carton labeling costs.
- Traveled to China four times to establish effective relations / communications; conducted in-depth study of the culture.
- Presently contribute to knowledge management team project exploring the use of Intranet technology.

LEAD CUSTOMER SERVICE REPRESENTATIVE (2000 – 2004)
Processed customer orders, coordinated product availability and shipments, and tracked sales. Worked extensively with freight brokers / forwarders in exporting shipments. Trained and coached new customer service reps. Led customer service rep team meetings and acted as key liaison with other departments.
- Designed international relationship supply chain management plan for new plants in China and Brazil, which led to the development of the Trade Desk Department.
- Promoted to develop and lead the new Trade Desk Team.
- Successfully managed development of export coordination to United Kingdom and Poland.
- Wrote department ISO documentation and work instructions.
- Helped establish company and department short-term goals as member of Quality Planning Team.

**PINZE DIE CASTING CO., INC.,** Burlington, Wisconsin          1995 – 1999
*Supplier of aluminum and zinc die castings with distinguished history of industry innovation and longevity.*
CUSTOMER SERVICE REP (1995 – 1999)
Processed customer orders, resolved issues, and collaborated with production department to ensure timely deliveries. Arranged plant production schedules with department managers when needed. Initiated and maintained quote tracking system. Established database for field representatives to access telemarketing information.

ACCOUNTS PAYABLE (1994 – 1995)

**BRETZEL INVESTMENT SERVICES, INC.,** Marshall, Wisconsin         1990 – 1994
BOOKKEEPER

**JAMES ASSOCIATES,** San Francisco, California         1988 – 1990
ACCOUNTING MANAGER

**ARLINGTON INSURANCE, INC.,** Sacramento, California         1985 – 1988
ACCOUNTING MANAGER

## Professional Development

CARDINAL STRITCH UNIVERSITY, Milwaukee, Wisconsin
**Bachelor of Business Administration,** 2008

INTERNATIONAL IMPORT – EXPORT UNIVERSITY, Dallas, Texas
**Certificate – Exporting / Importing Environment,** 2005
**Certificate – Documentation for the Global Marketplace,** 2005

# Mason Turner

7 O'Hare Drive • Newark, DE 19702
Phone: (302) 555-0003 • *mturner@yahoo.com* • Mobile: (302) 555-5181

## Product Manager / Senior Business Analyst & Strategist

Offering cross-functional sales, marketing, and business development skills; MBA with well-honed business acumen; and more than seven years of pharmaceutical experience, primarily with oncology market. Scope of experience encompasses pre-launch plans and execution strategies; alliance partnerships; strategic and tactile plans; quantitative and qualitative market research; product positioning; health care professional (HCP) opinion leader relations; employee training, mentoring, and development.

**Personal Formula for Success**

- *Strive relentlessly for customer excellence*: Actively seek to discover and meet needs of internal and external customers by building relationships and delivering innovative solutions.

- *Ensure commitment*: Stifle competing agendas and find common ground. Create shared vision by facilitating team communication, morale and effectiveness. Model and inspire trust and allegiance to company's best interests.

- *Strategically plan for success:* Dwell in possibility. Determine outcomes and establish benchmarks. Cut through the chaff and get down to business. Measure, analyze, and re-adapt.

- *Focus on delivery:* Manage multiple priorities and resources with appropriate sense of urgency. Take responsibility for redirecting efforts to deliver highest quality and productivity from self and others.

## Career Highlights

- Achieved aggressive upward career mobility from Pharmaceutical Sales Specialist to Business Analyst to Regional Alignment Manager—Made seamless transition from cardiology to oncology.

- Managed OmegaDanco's premier co-marketing agreement with small bioscience company while melding two distinctive business cultures and operational procedures to function as one. Leveraged existing vendor contacts to cut costs and maximize deliverables.

- Transformed marketing operations through highly effective business analysis, strategic planning, and execution to accelerate business opportunities.

- Created innovative solutions for compliance with speaker program management that resulted in $150K annual cost-savings.

- Played integral role in extensive pre-launch planning and successful delivery of *Luxor* to US marketplace. Leveraged sales specialist role to form unique communications link between brand team, sales representatives, and customers and ensure effective product positioning. Aggressively grew market share to 7% in six months.

## Professional Experience

**OmegaDanco Pharmaceuticals**, DE, MD & NJ                                     **2001 to Present**

*Regional Alignment Leader, Oncology*, Newark, DE (Jul 2007 to Present)

Collaborate with brand team, Regional Sales Director (RSD) and 10 District Sales Managers (DSM) to proactively identify market opportunity for oncology brands and develop road maps and benchmarks to assist sales team in transforming opportunities and capturing market share.

- Oversee community outreach programs, tap into cancer support networks, and align sales force initiatives with healthcare professionals to improve services to patients diagnosed with breast cancer.

- Lead collaboration with alliance partner team members to strategically develop, maintain, and manage HCP opinion leaders and ensure delivery of most effective messages to high-priority areas.

- As field promotions/local brand manager, identify opportunities and lead pull-through activities for reimbursement/access while ensuring field sales fully understand and appropriately utilize resources.

**Senior National Business Analyst, Oncology,** Philadelphia, PA (Jul 2006 to Jul 2007)

Key consultant to National Sales Director (NSD) and six RSDs on all oncology in-line brands. Developed and led successful execution of performance objectives and other key business strategies.

- Facilitated internal communication and built cohesion between brand directors and sales leadership to form united front in marketing products and interpreting results.

- Seized opportunity to groom newly hired regional business analysts for success by building oncology product knowledge through proactive leadership, training, and mentoring.

- Developed and led strategic targeting plan for cutting-edge alliance with small bio-pharmaceutical, managed business relations with internal and alliance sales professionals, and bridged communications between alliance business operations manager, NSDs, and RSDs.

- Championed customized approach to quarterly reviews of strategic targeting plans that minimized distraction rate and empowered PSSs and DSMs to focus on specialized business strategies.

**Regional Business Analyst, Oncology,** Newark, DE (Mar 2005 to Jul 2006)

Recognized for strong business acumen, peer leadership capabilities, and prior success in establishing physician-relations and chosen from pool of 30 applicants to lead business analysis activities targeting cardiovascular market—Within two months, made leap to oncology.

- Executed aggressive self-study initiatives and shadowed field sales representatives to quickly assimilate knowledge of oncology brands and drug development process.

- Performed analysis of current marketplace and emerging trends and opportunities. Collaborated with RSDs to develop and proactively adjust strategic plans to drive sales.

- Strengthened communication between PSSs, DSMs and RSMs and provided tools to allocate resources and secure funding. Transformed underperforming district and increased market share.

- Tagged by NSD to execute special projects. Developed and analyzed reports to track brand performance and provided motivation and focus that catapulted sales team to achieve market dominance.

- Simultaneously served as interim **District Sales Manager, Oncology** for Philadelphia, PA office (Jan 2006–Jul 2006). Led team of PSS promoting breast cancer and prostrate cancer products in PA market.

- Captured team confidence, eliminated internal discontent, and within four months accelerated team ranking for sales volume from 83 of 84 teams to second-place.

**Cardiovascular Sales Specialist,** Newark, DE (Sept 2001 to Mar 2005)

Promoted from business and sales administrative coordinator to join team of 10 PSS managing local territory. Promoted variety of pharmaceutical agents to specialists and primary care/internal medicine physicians. Contributed to successfully launching new brand.

- Built and nurtured mutually respected relations with no-access, large cardiology practice that resulted in fixed weekly appointments with 60% of practice physicians.

- Spearheaded monthly "book club" teleconferences with regional and district sales representatives to discuss current journal publications and maintain pulse on issues impacting healthcare providers.

- Championed customer-centered solutions for penetrating market by coaching, training, and developing new and existing sales representatives to overcome access challenges.

- Led divisional sales for new prescriptions and 2002 market-growth for *Atacand* and *Toprol XL*.

**Administrative Coordinator, BIS Sales,** Newark, DE (Feb 2001 to Sept 2001)

## EDUCATION

**M.B.A., Marketing, Saint Joseph's University,** Philadelphia, PA—Dec 2001

**B.S., Health Studies/Therapeutic Recreation, Temple University,** Philadelphia, PA—May 1998

# JAY WILEY, PMP

1234 Buchanan Street, Dallas, TX 75201
214-123-4567 • info@theresumestudio.com

*Record of Profit-Driven Technology Solutions Delivery*

Relocating to Los Angeles, CA

Creative, business-oriented, and technically sophisticated **Product Manager & Team Leader** with pioneering career leading to conversion rates of over 11 million registered members, 3.5 million simultaneous users, and revenues in excess of $32 MM. Cross-functional leader of up to 18 team members positioned globally in England, Australia, Mexico, and the United States. Development and calibration of forward-facing, first-in-class solutions.

**Cross Platform Internet Solutions / Customer Experience Guidelines & Help Desk Solutions**
**Team Leadership & Project Management / Creative Copywriting / Contract Negotiations / Vendor Relations**

## TECHNICAL PROFICIENCIES

**Web / Internet Design Operations & High Availability Client Service Environments:** Full complement of coding, design, integration, and IT planning experience. Able to quickly analyze and implement solutions and short term fixes while reinforcing long term initiatives, modernizing technical platforms, and promoting productivity.

- 24/7 Application Operations Support
- Project & Program Management
- User Experience Design / Support
- Legacy Systems Support

- HTML / CSS / JavaScript, PHP, ASP, SQL, JAVA, Crystal Reports
- Solution Requirements Development & Management
- Customer Relationship & Experience Management
- Agile / RUP Software Development Lifecycle Management

## EXPERIENCE

**MATCH.COM,** Dallas, TX (Headquarters)  |  *Serving 20 million registered users with $311 MM in 2007 revenues*

**Product Manager** *(12/04-present)* • **Usability Engineer** *(4/03-12/04)*
Hired to design and implement user experience solutions. Promoted to collaborate with peer divisions and lead employees and contractors in international development of business and functional requirements. Contribute to customer service processes and over 100 marketing campaigns annually. *Manage 2 direct reports and efforts of 20 team members. Report to CTO.*

**Product Feature Development**  |  *Competing in crowded social networking market, appealing to users 18-65*
- Released product enhancements that increased user base from 17.5 to 20 million plus in 12 months.
- Piloted company-wide integrated web redesign, formalizing design standards and information architecture.

**User Interface, Experience Design & CRM**  |  *Managing major market features and customer satisfaction*
- Increased weekly member signups from 15,000 to 19,000+ in three months.
- Led achievement of 96% first contact customer support resolution rate and average response time of under 21 minutes as daily support requests broke 3,500.
- Wireframed and produced standards-compliant product requirements documents for each of 120+ site pages, spanning over 12 functional areas.

**Leadership & Process Development**  |  *Innovative 12-month re-engineering of brittle and outdated codebase*
- Developed Change Control Board to promote interdepartmental transparency.
- Assigned task ownership to subject matter experts.
- Allocated resources between uninterrupted legacy product enhancements and new production baseline.

**SMITH INTERACTIVE,** Austin, TX | *The world's first technology-driven, interactive keychain*

**Professional Services Engineer** *(3/99-12/02)*
Project management support and technology implementation on behalf of Smith owners. Educated consumers; delivered job requirements and solutions; and integrated display of end-user reporting. Zero-hour backup reporting for system and user difficulties.

Envisioned technical workarounds to meet customer demands while using current technology stack; created first-generation solutions to increase revenues; introduced Crystal Reports and setup preliminary time-critical reports. Streamlined event setup and breakdown. Traveled 75% of time. *Managed temp staff remotely and in-house. Reported to Manager, Professional Services.*

- Improved core product reporting turnaround time by 10%.
- Increased Professional Services satisfaction scores by 40%.
- Improved Field Engineer customization time by 25%.
- Developed one-of-a-kind solutions to problems previously considered unsolvable.

**TUTORSTEACH.COM,** College Station, TX | *Tutoring, supplemental instruction, and group study*

**Project Manager** *(8/97-3/99)*
Consulting developer, managing hardware and software integration of startup technology stack. Launched first-in-class website, data management system, and scalable backend management architecture to integrate online bookings, appointments, and productivity reporting. *Reported to Director.*

- Radically improved data transfer for 100+ employees and 15,000-member student body.
- Reinforced legacy system, concurrently developing improvements and reducing support costs.

**CREATIVE TECHNOLOGY SOLUTIONS,** College Station, TX | *Technology consulting services*

**Consultant Lead Developer / Contractor** *(4/96-8/97)*
Recruited as lead developer to build Agency Management System for lead client, launching intuitive website serving 100 users and accomodating 250,000+ billing entries for 18,000+ client cases. Designed over 100 user reports; recruited and managed six vendors and two subcontractors; and increased user productivity by 150%+. *Reported to Project Sponsor.*

PROFILE ─────────────────────────────────────────

| | |
|---|---|
| Texas A&M University | Project Management Institute |
| College Station, TX | - **Project Management Professional** (PMP), 2004 |
| **B.A., Computer Science,** 1997 | |
| *Minor in Communications* | |

# Stan Wilson — Software Engineer

→110 – 45 Greenbriar Crescent → Toronto ON → M3H 3P3 →
→H. (416) 889-9938 → C. (416) 489-2938 → softwareguy@hotmail.com →

**Software Development**   **Project Management**   **Client Solutions**

## PROFESSIONAL PROFILE

Highly motivated software developer with strong programming skills and a talent for identifying and implementing innovative technology solutions that align with client objectives. Outstanding teamwork, problem-solving, and analytical skills using cutting-edge development tools and industry knowledge. Performs all tasks with precision and patience.

## TECHNICAL SNAPSHOT & TESTIMONIALS

| | |
|---|---|
| **Certifications:**<br>→ A+, MCSE, MCP, CCNA<br>**Operating Systems:**<br>→ Windows 2003/XP, Unix, Linux, DOS<br>**Programming Languages:**<br>→ JAVA, C/C++/C#/VC++, SQL 2000/2005, ASP.Net, Visual Studio.Net, Pascal | **Scripting Languages:**<br>→ HTML, XML, Java, CSS stylesheet<br>**Business Applications:**<br>→ MS Word/Excel/Visio<br>→ MS Outlook/Access/PowerPoint<br>→ HRMS/HRIS<br>**Hardware:**<br>→ PC, Printers, Hubs, Laptop, Routers |

*"I believe attitude and aptitude are the cornerstones of any organization and you have both of them. We need more Stan's in our company."* – A.B., President, Secure IT Inc.

*"Is there anything you can't fix? You are an IT wizard!"* – R.S., IT Director, Secure IT Inc.

## RELEVANT CAREER EXPERIENCE

**SECURE IT Inc., Toronto ON**      2006 to Present
*IT firm specializing in system security with locations worldwide.*
**Systems Engineer**
Selected to collaborate with client to define their requirements for infrastructure resources and implement agreed upon solutions. Responsible for operation of LAN and PC products.
*Noteworthy Accomplishments:*
→ Recognized by CEO for implementing conversion project resulting in a new $1M contract.
→ Designed new features for Panasonic's website increasing end user functionality by 40%.

**INNOVATE Inc., Toronto ON**      2004 to 2006
*Digital signage management firm specializing in brand infiltration with locations in North America.*
**Software Developer**
Hired to provide web programming services to a variety of clients including Samsung, Rogers, and Bell. Designed, built, and maintained websites and related software.
*Noteworthy Accomplishments:*
→ Supported a network for 2000+ users on LAN and WAN on a 365 X 24 X 7 basis.
→ Conducted time and motion study in manufacturing settings that indicated the amount of time spent by a machine operator before carrying out a productive motion.

## FORMAL EDUCATION

→ **Software Engineering Diploma,** SENECA COLLEGE, Toronto ON      2004
  o Made the Dean's list in 2003 & 2004.
  o Appointed by Director, IT Department as senior peer mentor for new students.

| 50140 Grim Drive | **JEFFREY L. ZIMMER** | Telephone: 703-555-1212 |
| Alexandria, VA 22304 | | Email: jzimmer@nhema.org |

## SENIOR ASSOCIATION MANAGEMENT EXECUTIVE

Fifteen-plus years' executive-level leadership and program development experience in membership-driven, non-profit organizations. Consistent record of success in delivering significant impact in financial management, member retention, educational programs and corporate sponsorships. Broad vision and perspective with focus on customer satisfaction. Excellent communicator who leads by example. Core competencies:

**Organizational Leadership & Planning – Board & Committee Liaison – Leadership Training – Policy Development**
**Regulatory & Legislative Affairs – Foundation Management – Member Services – Special Events Management**
**Program Development & Execution – Strategic Partnerships & Alliances – Conferences & Meetings**
**Staff Communication & Coaching – Sponsorships & Fundraising – Advocacy & Community Outreach**

### Executive Performance Milestones

<u>1989</u>: Assumed executive leadership of part-time association with 100 members and operating budget of $25K.

<u>1989 to 1997</u>: Successfully navigated organization's expansion in programs and services as secondary mortgage industry experienced huge growth.
- **Grew membership to all-time high with 370 members**, established headquarters in Washington DC, and added new government affairs department.

<u>1998</u>: Sustained organization's operations and services despite massive industry downturn and the loss of 50 corporate members.
- **Excess cash reserves built up during earlier growth years** help uphold organization during industry depression.

<u>1998 to 2000</u>: Executed tactical financial management techniques that helped propel organization back to operating status with sizable budget surplus.

<u>2001 to present</u>: Steered organization through continued industry transformations and membership cancellations as a large number of mortgage companies went through mergers.
- **Organization is recognized as industry leader** in the areas of educational conferences, topical seminars, and roundtable discussions.

### Key Organizational Leadership & Program Management Successes

**PRESIDENT** - National Home Equity Mortgage Association (NHEMA), Washington DC                1989 to present
*(Only trade association representing the non-prime mortgage lending industry with 250 members)*

**Grew organization from part-time association to fully staffed operations with over 100% increase in membership and an average annual budget in excess of $750K.** Provide strategic planning and direction for association's programs, activities and services. Full scope of responsibilities includes staff supervision, new program development, board and committee liaison, budget development, and member communications. Represent organization in legislative hearings before the Federal Reserve board and other trade committee meetings.

<u>**Financial Management & Budget Expansion**</u>:

Improved operational efficiency and financial stability by increasing member retention and sponsorship opportunities. Made pivotal decision to secure corporate sponsorships for annual conference and all other programs.

→ Drove cash reserves to an astounding $1.5 million during 1990's.

→ Stabilized organizational resources by capitalizing on sponsorship funds that now comprise 50% of annual income.

→ Promoted annual conference as largest sponsorship program and secured more than $400K in 2005.

**Member Services & Member Retention**:

Instituted proactive measures for membership renewals by contacting current members on continual basis to evaluate satisfaction and assess ongoing needs.

→ Member retention peaked consistently at 92-93% for 18 consecutive years.

**Educational Programming & Conferences**:

Expanded educational programs and meetings to wide cross-section of program events and services that adequate meet the changing needs of corporate leaders and executive members.

→ Established complete suite of programs including annual conference, fraud prevention and detection conference, legislative day, compliance and servicing roundtable, and attorneys' roundtable.

**Member Communications & Information Resources**:

Implemented cutting-edge communication tools to enhance member benefits and increase information sharing among members. Oversaw creation and publication of *Equity Magazine*, the member magazine and flagship communications vehicle for organization.

→ Promoted publication that now serves as revenue source for organization through paid advertisements from members and other industry experts.

**Website Development & Online Database**:

Brought organization to the forefront of industry by designing and developing company's first comprehensive website. Increased member benefits and visitor traffic to the website by including online database members with conference information, advocacy reports, and industry news.

→ Maximized revenue-generating opportunities by extending advertising space on company's website and weekly electronic newsletters to members.

**Foundation Development:**

Co-founded BorrowSmart Public Education Foundation in 2001; foundation provides potential borrowers and consumers with the knowledge, skills, and tools needed for financial literacy in the mortgage industry.

→ Established fundraising programs and raised more than $560K for first two years.

**Advocacy, Regulatory & Legislative Affairs**:

Channeled association to serve as advocate and lend powerful "voice" in legislative issues and regulatory affairs on behalf of members. Helped curtail excessive restrictions on member operations in the industry by advocating informed consumer choice, consumer education, and access to fairly priced credit.

→ Testified before Federal Reserve Board on matters related to home mortgage disclosure act and predatory lending.

## Education

BA – California State University Fullerton

JD – Pepperdine University

# Appendix C: Cover Letter Samples

The following fictionalized cover letters submitted by the professional resume writers listed in Appendix A showcase recommended strategies for designing strong cover letters to create a connection with the reader and encourage them to review the candidate's resume.

**Barbara Safani, MA, CERW, NCRW, CPRW, CCM**
Sample: *Kevin C. Sills*

**Ilona Vanderwoude, MRW, CCMC, CPRW, CJST, CEIP**
Sample: *Stephanie McCall*

**Rosa E. Vargas, NCRW, MRW**
Sample: *Erica Sweeney*

# KENNETH C. SILLS

44 President Street ◘ Brooklyn, NY 11215 ◘ 718-555-4343 ◘ kennethsills@gmail.com

June 1, 2008

Mr. James Sobel, CEO
Tech Solutions
134 Park Avenue
New York, NY 10016

Dear Mr.Sobel:

My former professor, Jason Rhodes, recommended that I contact you regarding your current opportunities for Knowledge Solutions and Business Solutions Consultants. With over five years of experience in IT business solutions roles, I strongly believe that my background meshes well with the needs of your organization.

In my current role at Smith & Blake Limited, I conduct extensive IT audits and needs assessments to optimize the operations infrastructure and improve customer servicing. In just one year I created a ticket tracking system to minimize problem resolution time, built operational scripts and flowcharts to streamline product delivery, recruited several members for the IT product delivery team, and wrote inaugural company policies and procedures.

Prior to my position at Smith & Blake, I was a technology consultant for IBM where I project managed an Exchange migration program for 20,000 users, rolled out a 6,000-seat NT/Exchange and Outlook initiative, trained hundreds of clients on PC upgrades, authored a "how to" repository for users, reduced error rates during migration projects by improving documentation, and significantly trimmed server down time and crashes by auditing server logs.

Excited by your opportunity and impressed by your company's services, I would welcome the chance to meet with you in person to discuss my qualifications in more detail. I am confident that I can add value to your business solutions team and I look forward to hearing from you. My resume is attached for your review. Thank you in advance for your consideration.

Sincerely,

Kenneth C. Sills

Attachment

# STEPHANIE MCCALL

8 Monahan Avenue  ·  Staten Island, NY 10373  ·  Home: (718) 209–1129  ·  Cellular: (646) 692–2298

August 11, 2007

Gloria Hinton
Chairperson Liberal Arts Dept.
Manhattan College
29 Fifth Avenue
New York, NY 10019

*"Wisdom begins in wonder."* – Socrates

Dear Ms. Hinton:

Creating an environment that generates enthusiasm from students and motivates them to retain knowledge is one of my strengths. As a teacher for 10+ years, I believe strongly in animated teacher-classroom interaction, presenting material in a style conducive to student participation and exploration. This philosophy, combining factual knowledge, creative teaching methodology, and a sincere love of teaching, has been key in my success as Adjunct Faculty at Queens College, New York, as a substitute lecturer at Baruch College, New York, and as an NYPD Instructor.

Subjects I am experienced in teaching are Criminal Justice, Public Administration, Political Science, Urban Affairs, Contemporary American History, and World Civilization. I have a master's degree in Political Science and I expect to start my doctoral studies in Urban Planning & Policy Development per September 2008.

In anticipation of Manhattan College's need for an educator with my background, I am enclosing my résumé outlining my qualifications and skills, highlights of which include:

- Recruited by Queens College to develop and implement new curricula for the Liberal Arts & Sciences Department.
- Interactive, animated, and motivational teaching style that led to "following of students".
- Conceptualize and orchestrate special events and lectures - including guest speakers - attracting students college-wide.
- Strong ability to quickly establish rapport with people from diverse backgrounds through extensive cross-cultural exposure as NYPD Sergeant. New York State certified in advanced communication and instruction techniques.

I would welcome a personal interview and will call you next week to follow up. Thank you for your time and consideration.

Sincerely,


Stephanie McCall

*Enclosure*

ERICA
SWEENEY

April 6, 2008

Ms. Medina
Nonprofit Organization
3799 Millenia Blvd
Orlando, Florida 32839

Dear Ms. Medina:

*How can I be useful, of what service can I be? There is something inside me, what can it be?*

*~ Vincent Van Gogh*

In 2008, I will graduate with an Associate's Degree in Human Services. My dedication is evident as I have held full-time jobs, raised children, and I am only a few credits away from graduation. I offer to service your not-for-profit organization with the same dedication. Kindly review my résumé for consideration.

With experience in a variety of service-oriented roles, my organizational skills, relationship building, trouble identifying and solving, judiciousness, and ability to focus on the larger picture, will be of benefit to your organization. I am highly reliable and flexible; have often been relied upon to work extra hours. Superiors always solicited my assistance in management and liaison roles; clients easily gravitate to me because I project professionalism, trust, and accountability.

*Positive contributions that I have made to my prior employers and now offer you:*

- **Strengthened communications** between employees, managers, and customers by advising co-workers, displaying a positive attitude, consulting clients, and embracing challenges.
- **Improved workflow and organization** by managing records, accounts, and securing compliance with policies and procedures.
- **Allocated more time for superiors** by working extra hours, learning everything possible, and rolling up my sleeves to aid management whenever there was lack.

Personally, I have always held an affinity for this field. It brings me great pleasure to help others; I understand the need for help and have always helped people locate venues, resources, and information to alleviate a life challenge, attain government, educational, medical, or financial help. I am very analytical and great at interpreting laws, guidelines, and complex documents. If there is a way to solve a problem—I will find it!

My family, co-workers, and friends have often referred to me as their personal social worker; little did I know I would eventually seek professional work in the not-for-profit industry

Thank you for your time. I look forward to meeting you in person and learning more about your organization.

Sincerely,

Erica Sweeney

3799 Amsterdam Ave | New York, NY 10025 | H: 212-555-5555 | C: 212-555-5555
Esweeney@email.com

# About the Author

**Barbara Safani,** owner of Career Solvers, has over twelve years of experience in career management, recruiting, and executive coaching. Barbara partners with both Fortune 100 companies and individuals to deliver targeted programs focusing on resume development, job search strategies, on-line identity, networking, interviewing, and salary negotiation skills.

Barbara has appeared as a career expert on CNN, ABC, FOX, and ROBtv and her career advice has been featured in The Washington Post and MSNBC online. She is a career consultant for CareerBuilder and she regularly contributes career-relevant content to The Ladders 100K Job Board and Kennedy Executive Agent.

Barbara holds a Master of Arts degree in Organizational Psychology from Columbia University and a Bachelor of Arts degree in Psychology from the State University of New York at Albany. She is certified by the Career Management Alliance, the National Resume Writers' Association, the Professional Association of Resume Writers, and Career Directors International, a distinction only a handful of resume writers world-wide have achieved. In addition, she is a three-time award winner in the TORI (Toast of the Resume Industry) annual awards competition sponsored by Career Directors International.

# Recommended Happy About® Books

Purchase these books at Happy About
http://happyabout.info
or at other online and physical bookstores.

### *Internet Your way to a New Job*

From selecting the most effective
tools, to proven methodologies
and expert perspectives,
this book will prepare you
to enter a competitive job
market with cofidence.

Paperback: $19.95
(with 15% discount only $16.96)
eBook: $11.95

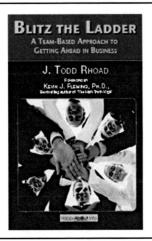

### *Blitz The Ladder*

Unique approach to improve your
career 'Blitz the Ladder' Will
provide you an in-depth view
at a unique approach to
improving your career.

Paperback: $19.95
(with 15% discount only $16.96)
eBook: $11.95

LaVergne, TN USA
09 February 2010

172479LV00009B/27/P